SECRETS

of

SPACE
CLEARING

ALSO BY DENISE LINN

Books

Altars

Dream Lover

Energy Strands

*Feng Shui for the Soul**

*Four Acts of Personal Power**

*The Hidden Power of Dreams**

*If I Can Forgive, So Can You**

*Kindling the Native Spirit**

*The Mystic Cookbook
(with Meadow Linn)**

*Past Lives, Present Miracles**

*Quest
(with Meadow Linn)**

Sacred Space

The Secret Language of Signs

*Secrets & Mysteries**

*Soul Coaching®**

*The Soul Loves the Truth**

Space Clearing

*Space Clearing A–Z**

*Unlock the Secret Messages of Your
Body!**

Oracle Cards

*Gateway Oracle Cards**

*Kindling the Native Spirit**

Sacred Destiny Oracle

Sacred Traveler Oracle Cards

*Soul Coaching® Oracle Cards**

Audio Programs

Angels! Angels! Angels!

Cellular Regeneration

*Complete Relaxation**

Dreams

*Journeys into Past Lives**

Life Force

Past Lives and Beyond

Phoenix Rising

*33 Spirit Journeys**

The Way of the Drum

Video

*Instinctive Feng Shui
for Creating Sacred Space**

*Available from Hay House
Please visit:

Hay House USA: www.hayhouse.com®
Hay House Australia: www.hayhouse.com.au
Hay House UK: www.hayhouse.co.uk
Hay House India: www.hayhouse.co.in

SECRETS
of
SPACE
CLEARING

Achieve Inner
and Outer Harmony
through Energy Work,
Decluttering,
and Feng Shui

DENISE LINN

HAY HOUSE, INC.
Carlsbad, California • New York City
London • Sydney • New Delhi

Published in the United States by: Hay House, Inc.: www.hayhouse.com®
Published in Australia by: Hay House Australia Pty. Ltd.: www.hayhouse.com.au
Published in the United Kingdom by: Hay House UK, Ltd.: www.hayhouse.co.uk
Published in India by: Hay House Publishers India: www.hayhouse.co.in

Cover design: Jordan Wannemacher • *Interior design:* Bryn Starr Best
Interior illustrations: Louis Zimmerman

Some of the material in this book has appeared in a modified form in *Space Clearing* (London: Contemporary Books, 2000) 0-8092-9739-6.

Library of Congress Cataloging-in-Publication Data

Names: Linn, Denise, author.
Title: Secrets of space clearing : achieve inner and outer harmony through
   energy work, decluttering, and Feng shui / Denise Linn.
Description: 1st edition. | Carlsbad : Hay House, Inc., 2021.
Identifiers: LCCN 2020044740 | ISBN 9781401961534 (trade paperback) | ISBN
   9781401961541 (ebook)
Subjects: LCSH: Mind and body. | Self-care, Health. | Energy medicine. |
   Feng shui.
Classification: LCC BF161 .L56 2021 | DDC 128/.2--dc23
LC record available at https://lccn.loc.gov/2020044740

Tradepaper ISBN: 978-1-4019-6153-4
E-book ISBN: 978-1-4019-6154-1
Audiobook ISBN: 978-1-4019- 6159-6

10 9 8 7 6 5 4 3 2
1st edition, January 2021

Printed in the United States of America

To the splendid James Everest Linn. . . .
May you always be surrounded with sacred space.
Remember sacred space is safe space.
May you be a safe space for others in the years ahead.

CONTENTS

INTRODUCTION

The Sacred Act of Space Clearing

Every space has energy. Your home is not only a combination of materials assembled for shelter. Every cubic centimeter of it, whether solid or seemingly empty space, is composed of infinite energy. When you enter a space that makes you immediately feel light or uplifted, or walk into a room where the atmosphere leaves you feeling depleted or drained, you are responding to the energy of the environment. If you notice tension and heaviness in a room after an argument has taken place, you are experiencing a residual energy that can linger in a room long after the argument has ended.

Sometimes energy in a home or office can become stagnant and dull. When this is the case, you may feel tired and listless, or become agitated and angry. However, learning a few simple techniques to cleanse the energy of your home can produce a remarkable and positive influence on the way you feel and on every aspect of your life.

THE ORIGINS OF SPACE CLEARING

For over 50 years, I have practiced the art of cleansing and harmonizing home energy, a skill that I named "space clearing"; some people call it home healing, smudging, or home harmonizing. No matter what name is used, present-day space clearing techniques have their source in ancient techniques practiced throughout human history. The methods and tools have varied from one culture to another, but the intent has been the same—to create greater harmony and balance.

Native Americans use drums, rattles, and burning herbs in their rituals. Some Chinese traditions use gongs, chanting, and incense. In medieval Europe, salt and prayers cleared energy, and in the Middle East, smoldering resins such as frankincense and myrrh were used to invite blessings into a home. Some of these traditions have survived virtually unchanged in modern times. The priest swinging an incense censer in a church and the person who throws salt over the shoulder to avert evil are both employing ancient techniques of space clearing, but many more have been lost to time.

These ceremonies that brought vitality to human structures generations ago are once again being used to instill peace and equilibrium in today's homes and businesses. Burning herb bundles has become so mainstream that you can often find supplies at your local health-food store. Many people are finding that these ancient rituals can be adapted very successfully for modern-day use; most important, they are discovering that they work.

Traditional Western businesses are hiring professional space clearers because they have found that doing so increases their sales and productivity. Some of the largest real estate firms are now using the services of space clearers in order to dramatically accelerate property sales. Land management corporations are employing space clearers to perform blessings on land before they build housing developments. People who had never heard of space clearing a year ago are now ringing bells, burning herbs, and chanting mantras because they have found that their homes feel better as a result.

SHARING MY DISCOVERIES WITH YOU

My passion for space clearing comes from the elders in numerous native cultures throughout the world with whom I have spent time and studied. In every culture, these wise wisdom keepers shared with me the immense value of clearing one's personal space and living environment. In addition, I have studied feng shui from various perspectives and wrote the second book in English about feng shui. I have been privileged to be taught space clearing by the Maori in New Zealand, the Aborigines in Australia, the Zulu in Africa, a Brazilian shaman, Lapland healers in Finland, and Native Americans, including those from my own Cherokee heritage.

As I began space clearing in homes and businesses, I came to realize that even small changes can have a profound effect on the energy of your environment and anyone who dwells within it. You don't need to perfect the feng shui of a space while doing space clearings in order to have an effect. Something as simple as clearing clutter with intention can profoundly transform your life in mystical ways.

As I moved deeper and deeper into my personal space-clearing journey, it seemed to me that one of the most powerful tools for cleansing and blessing a space was the body. I realized that our bodies could serve almost like lightning rods to receive, distill, magnify, and radiate life force energies.

As a result of this realization, I created unique *mudras*, sacred hand and body movements, to bless and seal energy in a living or work space. These movements are not something I learned from others. Instead, they came from my dreams and from a deep place of inner knowing within me. Every mudra seemed to emerge like a flower opening to the sun.

When I showed others how to do these mudras, the spaces they cleared would sparkle with vitality. Even more remarkably, it seemed that the same healing energy flowing outward was also flowing inward to reflect on the person doing the clearing. In other words, when you use these mudras, you'll find that your body, your home, and your life are healed as well!

I then discovered that the power of each mudra was magnified through connecting with the plant kingdom and utilizing plant resins, flowers, and essential oils from various plants. It was as if the mudras activated the plant energies, and in turn the plants magnified the mudra.

The results from combining mudras and oils have been remarkable. I felt Spirit beside me as this system, which I call Elemental Space Clearing®, unfolded in my heart. It's an honor to share my discoveries about space clearing, including Elemental Space Clearing, and clutter clearing with you in this book.

How This Book Is Set Up

In this comprehensive book, you will learn the secrets of space clearing using different tools and methods as well as ceremonies that you can adapt to your own specific needs.

Part I is a broad introduction to space clearing. Chapter 1 offers an overview of energy and the best times to do a space clearing. Chapter 2 breaks down the four stages of space clearing. Chapter 3 delves into specific techniques and other ways you can prepare yourself and your space for a clearing. Chapter 4 demonstrates how the act of clearing clutter can go beyond just getting rid of things and instead be a transformative process. Chapter 5 guides you through the energy of each room that you'll experience as you clear a space.

Part II, Chapter 6 through 9, offers a deeper dive into the tools and techniques you'll use while space clearing, covering vibrational energy (sound), fire, air, water, and earth. Chapter 10 explains Elemental Space Clearing® in the context of all you've just learned and introduces you to the mystic mudras.

Through this book, you will learn all you need to know to clear the energy of your home or business. You will also learn a bit about feng shui, although not in the traditional Chinese form. Instead, you will gain an intuitive understanding that every space has energy and that energy affects our lives. This will deepen your understanding of space clearing as, throughout history, space clearing has always been an integral part of feng shui; the two go hand in hand. (If you're interested in learning more about feng shui, see my books *Feng Shui for the Soul* and *Sacred Space*.)

The most important requirements for any clearing will always be your own intuition and the promptings of your heart. As you open your heart to Spirit, you will be led to the tools, the information, and the ceremonies that are right for you. It is my intent that this book will get you started on that path, so that your house will be a place that you love to come home to and where you feel a deep sense of peace.

If you feel like you'd like to dive in even deeper into space clearing or clutter clearing (perhaps find a certified practitioner— or even become one yourself!), please visit the Recommended Resources section of this book to learn more.

The work of space clearing is profoundly sacred to me, and it's an honor to share it with you. I'm excited for you to see the enormous impact space clearing can have on every aspect of your life. The human psyche responds dramatically and powerfully to symbolic acts. Be observant and tune in to yourself as you work through this book. Powerful, profound shifts will occur deep beneath the surface. Your life and your energy field are being cleared and subsequently blessed. When you call for blessings and assistance from the unseen realm of Spirit in your space clearing, untold magic and joy can fill your heart so that your house becomes a home for your soul.

PART I

Space
Clearing
Fundamentals

CHAPTER 1

Space Clearing Practices

The shaman slowly reaches forward to light the incense. As smoke fills the air, he begins a sonorous chant. The rising and falling of his voice seems to undulate throughout the room. Wave after wave of low humming tones flow from him, resonating in every niche and corner of the space. The soft beating of a drum accompanies his chant as he stands to face each of the four directions, asking for blessings for the home and all its occupants. In each direction he prays to the Creator for good health, prosperity, and love for all. The smoke settles. The drumming subsides. Everyone smiles. Good fortune will reign in this home.

REBIRTH OF AN ANCIENT TRADITION

For thousands of years, in ancient civilizations and cultures throughout the world, sacred ceremonies have been performed to instill beneficial energy in living spaces. Although many of these traditions have withered in the climate of our modern, technology-driven world, arising from the deep wisdom of the earth comes the rebirth of space clearing. Forgotten ceremonies that once brought vitality to human structures generations ago are now more commonly known and used to establish peace and equilibrium in today's homes and businesses with remarkable results. Homes that felt sluggish or depressing become vibrant and uplifting after a space clearing. Stores and offices that have been cleared often report an increase in sales and morale. A room that is cleansed feels at once lighter and brighter—and even people not sensitive to energy remark how great they feel.

Space clearing today can provide keys to inviting the natural world into our homes. It can reveal the spiritual possibilities lying dormant in our surroundings, dispel negative energy, and call Spirit and love into our homes and businesses. A home that has been purified not only feels better but sometimes, in seemingly mystical ways, we find that health improves, relationships deepen,

3

and prosperity expands. Ancient people understood the power of cleansing and blessing their homes and living structures, and this is why space clearing was such an important part of their everyday life.

The journey to understanding space clearing (and learning how it can make a difference in your home) lies in the realm of energy. Our homes are not just inanimate physical structures. They are receptacles for vibrating unseen energy fields that respond to human thought and intention. In this book I have sought to unravel some of the mysteries of energy and space clearing to show you how, when it has been cleared, the house becomes an environment of spiritual revival and inner poise.

WHEN SPACE CLEARING IS NEEDED

Space clearing can be done at any time, yet there are particular instances when it is especially important to clear and bless your environment. The type of clearing you do will depend on the history of the space and what has occurred there.

For example, after a sickness or death of a loved one, the energy of a home often becomes sluggish and heavy, or *yin* in nature. To dispel the listless energy and restore balance in the area, clearing techniques that are vibrant and quick moving are required—these are *yang* (active) in nature. Drums and gongs are excellent tools to use in such a case.

On the other hand, if the energy of your space feels continually agitated, to create an oasis of peace you might choose to use techniques and tools of a yin quality. The use of a crystal singing bowl or softly chanted mantras can create tranquility and calm.

Before Construction of a New Home

In ancient traditions, it was considered a sacrilege to begin the construction of a building before clearing and consecrating the land. Anecdotal evidence supports the validity of this belief, as homes built on battle sites or hallowed ground have often been plagued by continuous problems. Simply taking the time to connect and communicate with the earth, clear the land of residual energy, and offer blessings can make an enormous difference in the fortunes of all the occupants of a home. Blessings for the land forge a symbolic link between the house and the life-giving earth it rests upon. The occupants of this home will reap the benefits of living in this location.

Before Moving into a Home

In many cultures it was unthinkable to move into a home that hadn't been space cleared and blessed. Homes that have not been freed of residual energies will sometimes continue to foster patterns of behavior related to the emotions of the previous occupants. If there was a lot of anger experienced by previous owners, this can create an energy echo called residual energy. Residual anger in a home can make it easier for the current residents to have anger issues.

Also, it is not uncommon for a business to go bankrupt in a building that has seen previous bankruptcy. Although this could be attributed to a bad location, it is more likely that the negative energy created by the previous misfortune created a template for failure; this is called predecessor energy.

Even if the previous homeowners were healthy and happy, it is still advantageous to clear the space so you're free to create your own traditions and space there. You'll then be surrounded by your own energy rather than someone else's.

After Misfortune

It's absolutely essential after illness, divorce, death, or misfortune that you space clear your home. Doing this facilitates the timely release of pain, suffering, sorrow, and discomfort, so that you can begin anew. It will literally help to "clear the air" of stagnant, unhealthy, negative, or unhappy energy. Also, space clear your home after arguments, home accidents, or the departure of an unpleasant visitor.

Anytime You Need a Lift

You can also do space clearing anytime you need a lift in life. Have you been feeling sluggish or lackluster? If so, this would be an excellent time to perform a space clearing ceremony. Although a complete clearing involves an entire home or office, even the simple act of lighting a candle, misting a room, or ringing a bell will have a positive effect on how you feel, if it is done with the intent of transforming the energy in your environment.

You may want to do a light space clearing every morning to start your day with crisp, clear energy. Simply walking around each major room in your home ringing a bell, lighting incense at an altar, or wafting the smoke of an herbal bundle with a feather in the morning hours can set a template of clarity for the rest of the day.

Before a Celebration or Rite of Passage

Space clearing before bringing a new baby home, the arrival of an honored guest, or a rite of passage such as a marriage ceremony in the home sets a template of clarity and light. It creates a perfect environment for generating fresh new beginnings.

THE BEST TIMES TO SPACE CLEAR

Annual Spring Clearing

It is valuable to cleanse and purify the energy of your home at least once a year. This will "set" the energy for the coming year. Ideally, this complete clearing is done either at the winter solstice or in very early spring. Both times are auspicious for new beginnings.

In the springtime, as new life abounds, clarify your goals and dreams for that coming year, then thoroughly purify your home and office, top to bottom, to create a powerful template for the coming year. Your space clearing ritual creates an energy that will continue to feed and nourish your home for the coming year.

The Most Auspicious Time of Day

Space clearing can be done at any time of day or night; however, the early morning hours (especially after a waxing full moon the night before) offer the freshest and most potent energy. Opening windows and allowing morning sunshine to stream in during a clearing can invite beneficial vibrant energy into a dwelling.

In some Eastern European traditions, space clearings are often done at night during the dark of the moon. In these countries, it is believed that disturbing or negative home energy is at an ebb at that time, so in theory it is easier to set a new energy in place. However, the best time to do a clearing is when it feels right to you.

CHAPTER 2

The Four Stages of Space Clearing

When you cleanse and purify the energy in your home, it becomes a sanctuary—a retreat from the discord of the world, a place of refuge and protection. It becomes an anchoring point from which you venture out into the world as well as a welcoming abode for your return. A home that has been cleansed and blessed becomes somewhere you feel safe enough to be yourself, a place to embrace your joy and explore your pain. Space clearing can turn every inch of a home into a sanctuary of sacred space that nurtures the soul.

It's important to note that there is no single "right" way to do a space clearing ceremony. It is your prerogative to customize your ceremonies with specific tools and techniques that are right for your needs. The chapters that follow are dedicated to giving you all the information needed to empower you to make your choices with confidence and wisdom.

The space clearing ceremonies and specific tools described in this book can be used in the context of the four stages of space clearing:

1. Preparation
2. Purification
3. Invocation
4. Preservation

When followed with care and love, these steps will bring balance into your home and life. They create a powerful integration of your outer life and your inner life.

STAGE 1: PREPARATION

There are several steps that need to be taken well in advance of a space clearing and some that you will do on the day of. The following are a quick overview of the steps that you will take to prepare for a space clearing. Chapter 3 will offer more detailed information and specific techniques.

1. *Clarify your intention:* The first step is getting clear on your and the other participants' intentions for the space clearing. Without this step, the space clearing is ineffective. Talk to the other members of the household (if there are any) about their intention for themselves and the home. Focus on the results you desire for the home, the other occupants, and yourself. Do this well in advance of when you plan to do the clearing, so you can have the proper tools ready.

2. *Prepare the space:* The most powerful space clearing occurs in a place that has been physically cleaned and cleared of clutter.

3. *Check in with yourself:* It is important that you feel emotionally balanced when space clearing. If you feel any apprehension or fear, you should postpone your clearing until you feel confident and relaxed.

   If you are pregnant or menstruating, you need to tune in to yourself to see if your energy is right for space clearing. A woman's moon time and pregnancy are times when her energy naturally turns inward. When doing space clearing, you need to project energy outward.

4. *Activate your intuition:* On the morning of your clearing, meditate for a few minutes on the task before you. Sit quietly, close your eyes, and visualize the home space as joyous, shimmering, and light.

5. *Protect yourself:* From a spiritual perspective, there is nothing out there that isn't you. That is, you are truly *one* with all things. We are a part of all things and to the extent that you experience this, there is nothing that can harm you and there is no need for protection. It is not uncommon when space clearing to enter this state, in which case you do not need protection.

However, there are occasions when it is essential to cloak your energy field so that you can be more effective in your space clearing. You should not hesitate to protect yourself if you feel the need. Specific techniques are included in Chapter 3.

6. *Cleanse yourself:* Before you purify and bless a dwelling, it is essential that you cleanse yourself. If possible, bathe or shower before a clearing and wash your hair. If you can't wash your hair, then at least stroke water over the top of your head. This traditional cleansing of the top of the head allows for an unclouded connection between you and Spirit.

7. *Set up your tools and Blessing Altar:* At the beginning of your ceremony, you can either arrange your space clearing tools and altar objects in silence, or you can say a blessing for each item. (Guidance for choosing tools and creating a Blessing Altar is given in Chapter 3.)

8. *Call for spiritual assistance:* After you have arranged the Blessing Altar, take a moment to center your thoughts. Then, either in your inner thoughts or aloud, open your heart and call for spiritual guidance. State your intention and ask for blessings for the home. The words you use are less important than your intent. Angels, spirit guides and guardians, ancestors, and totem allies will respond and send beneficial healing energy when prayers are sent straight from the heart.

The Blessing Altar

A Blessing Altar is created by arranging objects on an altar cloth that will be used in your clearing rites. You can choose the colors, objects, etc., for each altar, depending on the goals of a particular space clearing ceremony.

Creating a Blessing Altar is perhaps the single most important aspect of space clearing. It provides a spiritual backdrop so that every action has meaning and power. The ceremonies performed within this sacred space deepen the overall effect of your space clearing. In no small way, the altar mystically magnifies every part of your clearing and blessing and also serves as a kind of beacon to "call" spiritual assistance and then radiate sparkling energy into the space.

The Blessing Altar serves as a beginning point and ending point for your ceremony and has three purposes:

1. It initiates energy for the clearing. It is here where you will call upon spiritual assistance and support.

2. It acts as a kind of beacon that radiates a protective, loving energy throughout the home during the entire space clearing.

3. It anchors, grounds, and integrates the new energy that has been generated by your clearing ceremony.

I'll discuss how to set up your Blessing Altar and the ceremonies you'll perform at it in Chapter 3.

STAGE 2: PURIFICATION

The second step of your space clearing is purification. In this stage, you are releasing negativity and clearing out old energy. When energy is cleared, the room might look bigger, colors are brighter, corners are sharper, sounds are clearer, the air smells great, and your body feels uplifted. These are the steps to do this:

1. *Place tools on your Blessing Tray:* At the completion of your prayers at the Blessing Altar, slowly and deliberately place any tools you will be using on a small, portable tray. This is your Blessing Tray, which you will be carrying with you, room to room. Any kind of tray can be used as long as it provides a stable surface for your items and is easy to carry. Pick it up and place it in the room that you are going to clear.

2. *Attune:* Stand at the entrance of the room that you are going to clear and take a few minutes to be still to attune to the space. Radiate your intention into the room and send prayers to the Creator for guidance and assistance.

3. *Sensitize your hands:* Breathe slowly and deeply. Sense the energy of the space. Circle the room with your hands extended, or use any of your senses to perceive the energy in the room.

4. *Break up the stagnant energy:* Using the tools that you have chosen, gradually break up the stagnant energy of the room. (If you are doing an Elemental Space Clearing, your tools will be your essential oils and mudras.) As a general rule, circle the room clockwise in the Northern Hemisphere and counterclockwise in the Southern Hemisphere. If your intuition directs you otherwise, listen to it. (In Mecca, for instance, pilgrims go counterclockwise around their sacred stone enshrined in the Kaaba. Buddhists walk clockwise around stupas, or shrines.)

5. *Smooth the energy of the space:* After you have cleared a room, be sure to smooth the energy of the space. To do this, you can run your hand gently around the periphery of the room, just as though you were petting a cat, until you sense that it feels settled and smooth. (You can also use a tool to smooth the energy.)

6. *Seal the room:* You'll complete your clearing of a room at the spot where you first began. Make a figure eight with your tool or with your hands to seal the circle. You can also seal the room with a flower offering (see box on next page).

Remember to silence your mind and go slowly with each step of purification. This allows you to perceive subtle energy flows.

You'll move from room to room with your Blessing Tray. Generally, you'll want to work your way from the bottom floors to the top floors, as this directs the energy upward.

Flower Offerings

Flower offerings are a lovely way to seal the energy of each room once you have finished clearing it. They are a simple and elegant expression of love, beauty, and Spirit. These beautiful offerings are also a way of giving thanks to the Creator and the spirit guardians for all the love and assistance they have given to your home. They honor the four sacred elements. Incense honors the Spirit of Air, flowers acknowledge the Spirit of the Earth, a candle represents the Spirit of Fire, and holy water venerates the Spirit of Water.

To make a flower offering, follow these steps:

- Place a small tea light candle (the type in small metal containers) in the center of a heat-resistant plate, saucer, or dish on your Blessing Tray. (Make sure that no flammable materials or curtains are nearby.)

- Arrange your chosen flowers around the candle. Use colors and flowers that are appropriate to your overall intention. (See Appendices A and C.)

- To energize your arrangement, take the head of one flower and use it to gently sprinkle holy water over the other flowers in the offering. (For instructions on how to make holy water, see Chapter 8.) You can also place a stick of incense in an incense holder next to the offering. (For guidance in choosing incense, see Chapter 7.)

- Once you are done clearing a room, leave the offering in a place where it will not be disturbed by children or animals. Ideally, these offerings should be left in all the major rooms of the home after a space clearing for at least 24 hours. If desired, they can be left longer.

- When you are done with your offerings, return them to nature. You can place them in an inconspicuous part of your garden or add them to your compost heap. In this way, you let them complete their natural cycle. As you do so, remember to offer a prayer of thanks for the "giveaway" that they have provided.

STAGE 3: INVOCATION

The invocation and blessing stage in a space clearing ceremony entails calling on a higher power for assistance, support, and inspiration for filling a living space with blessings. If we liken the purification stage of space clearing to washing a dirty vase, the invocation stage could be compared to placing beautiful fresh flowers in the vase. Here are the steps for this:

1. *Invoke blessings:* After a room is cleared, imagine that it is filled with light and love, while asking for support and guidance from the spiritual realms. Pray silently or aloud as you do so. You can circle the room again while doing this, or simply invoke energy into the space from the door where you completed your purification stage. (See the box "Flower Offerings" on page 15 for a ritual you can do at this stage.)

2. *Bless each household member:* When you have completed all the rooms, cleanse and bless each household member. This is essential because it aligns their energy with the newly cleansed energy of the home.

3. *Perform completion blessings:* Return to the Blessing Altar. Offer thanks and ask for good fortune for the home and all its occupants and visitors. This is the completion blessing ceremony, one of the most important aspects of the clearing; it must be done with reverence, respect, and devotion. The time and energy you spend at the end of the ceremony integrate the energy of the space clearing you have just performed.

4. *Put your tools away:* With the same deliberate care you took while laying out your altar, place all your space clearing tools away. You may cleanse them now or do so later, but don't store them without cleansing them first. Offer gratitude and love for the service of each item.

5. *Wash your hands:* Wash with cool water all the way to the elbows. Shake a few times before you dry your hands.

STAGE 4: PRESERVATION

Once you have purified a space and blessed it, do the following to preserve the wonderful energy that you have created:

1. *Bathing:* It is essential that everyone, including you and all members of the household, should bathe within six hours after the space clearing. Doing this not only cleanses the body but also symbolically refreshes the spirit and helps preserve the energy you have created in your home. A simple bath or shower with a cold rinse is fine, but bathing in saltwater is especially beneficial.
   Salt bath: Dissolve ½ pound (8 oz.) of regular salt or Epsom salt in the bathwater.
   Salt shower: Rub your body with salt before showering, ending with a cold rinse.

There are a few other methods from which you can choose to further sustain the energy:

- *Planting a prayer:* Write a prayer or blessing on a piece of paper during your completion at the Blessing Altar and bury it in a favorite plant in the home. Every time the plant is watered, the prayer will be symbolically energized.

- *Symbols:* Draw a symbol or write a special word on a stone, then tuck it away by the front door, by a plant, or in an elevated place in the home.

- *Stones:* Leave a stone (or several stones) in a special place in the house to radiate energy. (See Appendix B for guidance on choosing stones.)

- *An object from the Blessing Altar:* Place an object from the Blessing Altar such as a figurine of an angel, a crystal, or some other representation of the divine realms in a special place in the home.

- *Oil blend:* If you made a special essential oil blend for the clearing, you can put it into a small mister, burner, or diffuser. This is an easy way to renew the wonderful energy that was instilled during the ceremony at a later time.

SIMPLE CEREMONY FOR PROTECTION FOR A HOME

This simple protection ceremony can be helpful for soothing the energy of a home in addition to space clearing. Intention is key for this ceremony.

- Start at the front door. Become relaxed and centered.

- Light and hold a candle.

- Look into the flame of the candle and imagine the light expanding and enveloping you in an orb of light.

- As you hold the candle near the center of your chest, infuse it with love. Move the candle upward to the heavens. As you move it down in a straight line in front of you, imagine bringing light into your home and say, "Safe, protected, and well." Return the candle to the center of your chest. Now move the candle to the left and then move it in a horizontal line to your right and say, "Safe, protected, and well." The vertical and horizontal lines form a cross that is sacred and protective. The cross is a holy symbol of peace and protection.

- Continue through the home, going from bottom to top in a clockwise direction. At every outside door and window make a cross and say, "Safe, protected, and well."

- Return to the front door. Repeat the cross and say, "Safe, protected, and well." This completes the ritual. Blow out your candle.

CHAPTER 3

Setting *the* Groundwork *for* Space Clearing

The success of any journey depends on the attention given to preparations made at its outset. There is immense power in beginnings, for as the seed is nurtured, so grows the tree. Taking the time to prepare yourself, your tools, and the space you are clearing will dictate how powerful the transformation will be.

The techniques described in this chapter are safe for everyday use in your home. However, do *not* attempt advanced techniques, such as the release of an earthbound spirit, until you've had further training and experience. (See the Recommended Resources or visit www.deniselinn.com.)

PREPARING YOURSELF

The strength of your space clearing depends on your ability to intuitively sense energy, clarify your intention, and project your will into a space. There are a few exercises you can do every day to continue developing your intuition and ability to sense energy.

Develop Your Intuition

Your intuition is the key that will open the door into the revealing world of energy in your home or business. All space clearing has its roots in shamanism, and shamanism has its basis in attunement to the natural cycles of nature. So, to develop your intuition, spend time outdoors. Lie on the earth. Feel her energy radiate through your body. Look up to the heavens. Watch the clouds as they form and reform above you. Notice any signs or messages in what you see. Doing this exercise helps you develop your intuition for perceiving the hidden messages indoors in houses or businesses.

Another way to develop and prepare your intuition is to spend time being absolutely still in nature. Only when you learn to silence your thoughts can your inner voices be heard, and this is easier in a natural environment.

Develop Your Awareness of Energy

One of the skills necessary for space clearing is the ability to sense energy fields. Developing this awareness is what will allow you to sense when energy is out of balance in a room and what changes need to be made in order to restore harmony.

To develop this skill, go around the periphery of a space very slowly with one hand extended outward. Notice places where you feel a difference. Your arm may feel heavy or light, or warm or cold in places. There may be places that seem to feel sticky and places that feel smooth. This is not your imagination. You are sensing energy. The secret is to slow down, still your mind, and trust what you are perceiving.

Clarify Your Intention

Where intention goes, energy flows. Before you begin any space clearing, as mentioned earlier, it is essential that you become very certain about what you hope to accomplish in a dwelling. The clarity and vigor of your intention will determine the direction and focus of the clearing. If your intention is to create a calming energy, this is what will occur. If you resolve that your space clearing will bring a dynamic vitality to a household that has been stagnant, then this will be the outcome.

If you are doing a clearing for another, you'll want to set up an interview so that you can understand the intentions of all involved. Ask a few questions: What do they want to release? What do they want to attract more of in their life? Make sure to listen more than you talk. Build a comfortable rapport.

Project Your Energy

The more chi (inner energy) you have, the more powerful your space clearing will be. When your chi is flowing, you can project your intention into a space magnificently and gracefully. To develop your chi, you might consider practicing meditation or taking tai chi or yoga classes.

An exercise to activate this unseen, yet very real inner life force is to imagine that you have a ball of energy in your hands. Slowly move this energy ball around. After a while you should feel an increasing sensation in your palms. This is your chi increasing.

A visualization to project your will into a space is to imagine that your body is a sacred vessel through which vast loving energies of the universe are pouring through your hands and into your home.

NAMING YOUR HOME

In your space clearing journey, you might consider naming your home. In many native cultures throughout the world, homes are named. Sometimes it's a sound rather than a word with a specific meaning, but most often it comes from nature. Naming comes from the belief that there is a living consciousness within each home, which becomes a kind of silent guardian and protector in a spirit of gratitude for being named.

A name is more than a label; it also speaks to an object's energy. Each name has a unique energy vibration, so it can help evoke specific qualities in that object. It also places intent and a purpose in the environment in which you dwell and can change how you vibrate within its space. It has been shown that people relate differently to each other because of their name—the same is true with you and your home.

It's important when naming your home to find a name that matches the essence of your home. One name isn't better than another; they just possess different energies.

A home that is named offers greater protection and security than one that is impersonal. Calling your home by its name will continue to increase the bond, connection, and vibrancy between you and your home. In this process of greeting your home, you awaken its vibrancy, which translates into your life as well.

Connect to the Essence of Your Home

When you space clear your home, it's valuable to first connect to its essence. You should feel at home with yourself in this space and feel at home in the universe. Connecting to the essence of your home will strengthen these feelings. You can do this anytime you feel like you need to check in with the energy in your home.

To do this exercise, close your eyes and relax. Imagine it is late at night and you are walking through your neighborhood. The lights are off and people are sleeping. As you stop in front of each house, use your inner sight to look through the walls. Inside each home you can perceive a luminous glow. You are sensing the seed energy, or core essence, of that home.

The seed energy of each dwelling may look different: one may be a radiant symbol such as a star; another may be undulating golden light. As you approach your home, imagine standing in front of it and noticing that within its walls is a luminescent light—its seed energy, its essence. Now visualize a strand of energy flowing from you to the essence of your house. This deepens your connection with your home and helps to make it a more nurturing place for you.

The seed energy of your home is like the chorus of a piece of music. It is a recurring motif that will appear again and again. Even though it may be slightly different each time it is heard, there will still be easily recognizable characteristics that give artistic unity to the piece as a whole.

The seed energy of your home captures its essence. When you connect with this energetic essence, you feel more at home when you are there. Every time you connect with the true essence of something, you deepen your connection to it.

MEDITATIONS YOU CAN DO
BEFORE A SPACE CLEARING

Consider doing any of the following meditations before a clearing to deepen your experience or gain added insight.

- *Connect with the spirit of your house:* Embark on a creative visualization meditation to meet the home and ask what it needs for itself and its residents.

- *Journey to your home:* Fly over it and see through the roof and walls to sense and see energy within, under, around, and above it; then call upon angelic beings and earth spirits to cleanse and infuse your home with energy and life force.

- *Journey to the earth beneath your home:* Talk to the Spirit of the Earth and the land beneath the home (notice sinkholes and underground water). See if the home is connected and integrated with the earth, or if is just sitting on the land, but not connected. A balanced home is one in which the Spirit of the Earth has grown into the house and the house has become a part of the earth.

- *Journey to the past:* Research the past to understand how predecessor energy and residual energy may be affecting the energy of your home. Imagine traveling to the far past, before the houses were there, before even people were there. What animals roamed the land? What plants and trees grew in the area? All of this influences the energy of the space. You can also call upon the oversouls of past and present animals, plants, trees, and stones to bring balance into the current home.

- *Journey to the future:* Sometimes what is needed in the present will be different from what is needed in the future. Ask the Spirit of the Future what will sustain the energy of your home in the years ahead.

Affirmations You Can Incorporate into Your Space Clearings

Affirmations are any statement said in the present tense that affirms your intent. An example of an affirmation you can say while space clearing is: "My home is filled with empowering energy, expanding love, and incredible life force." While most people are familiar with positive affirmations, it's important to note that negative statements can also be a kind of affirmation that can (unintentionally) attract more of an unwanted energy into your life.

Using affirmations while clearing each room will bring sparkling energy and intention within the space as the old energy is released. It might sound strange that this could change the feeling in a room, but try it—it works! Each room in your home has a specific purpose, and by using an affirmation that clearly states the purpose, you supercharge the energy of your clearing.

Consider some of the following ways that you might practice affirmations in your space clearing ceremony:

- Repeat affirmations to clarify your intention during the preparation stage.
- Write affirmations on slips of paper, candles, or other objects on your Blessing Altar.
- Chant affirmations at your Blessing Altar during the invocation stage.
- Write affirmations on the risers of your stairs to activate vibrant energy.

The following are examples of affirmations that you might take as inspiration to create your own:

- *For the bedroom:* My body and my life are nurtured and regenerated.

- *For the bathroom:* My body and my life are purified, cleansed, and healed. Sacred waters purify my life. I am refreshed and renewed.

- *For the front door:* I welcome joy and radiant life-force energy into my home.

- *For the kitchen or dining room:* I am nourished and nurtured in all areas of my life.

- *For the living room:* I relax in the knowledge of having excellent relationships with friends and family.

- *For the office:* I love my work. All that I do yields excellent results. Abundance flows into my life!

- *For the basement:* I am at ease with my past, and my past is clear and radiant.

- *For the attic:* I aim for higher realms.

PRACTICAL CONSIDERATIONS

The following are commonsense preparations to keep in mind before doing a space clearing.

Prepare the Space

Before any major space clearing, make sure that you go through every room, removing as much clutter as possible. For more information on clutter clearing, see Chapter 4.

In addition, do a thorough cleaning. Vacuum the rugs, mop the floors, wash the windows. Open the windows wide to allow sunshine and fresh air to fill the rooms. Put away any open containers of food, as they may absorb some of the energy being cleared.

Make sure arrangements are made to keep children and animals out of the working space on the day of the space clearing. The wagging tail of a friendly dog can send space clearing tools flying.

Carefully Choose Your Clothes for Space Clearing

The clothes you wear during a space clearing matter. They should be clean and carefully selected for the occasion. They can be of your choosing but should be appropriate to the situation and shouldn't be casual, everyday clothes. The colors of the clothes you wear are also important. Light colors reflect and dark colors absorb. During your clearing, it's best to reflect the energy rather than absorb it. See Appendix A for the qualities of colors that you might choose for your clothing.

It is best to remove jewelry, particularly rings and bracelets, as they can subtly impede your ability to sense energy. (This is optional; do so only if it feels right intuitively.)

Stay Hydrated

It is vital that you are properly hydrated before and after the space clearing. The water will help you transport energy through your body and release any unneeded energy that you may have taken on during the clearing.

PROTECTING YOURSELF

Should you protect yourself before a space clearing? There are compelling reasons on both sides of the debate. From a spiritual perspective, it's not always a good idea to protect yourself, for there is a mystical dimension within each of us wherein dwells the entire universe. It is a domain where you are not separate from the mountains, clouds, or great seas. Ancients, sages, and visionaries have spoken of this dimension with awe and reverence. On a very deep, spiritual level, there is nothing that is separate from you, so there is no need to protect yourself . . . because everything is "you."

As soon as you set up protection, you are defining some things as outside yourself and harmful. In a strange way, this makes what you deem as "bad" become even more so. It is a kind of polarization. What you resist persists. If you spend a lot of time and energy resisting "bad" energy and protecting yourself, you are creating the very things that you need to protect yourself from.

Those who constantly feel a need to protect themselves have a tendency to be a victim of life; often they may feel a lack of personal power. By continually repeating rituals for protection, they are actually defining themselves as helpless and affirming their own powerlessness. It's important to be aware of this.

However, as most of us don't experience a beneficent state of grace on an ongoing basis, and as it is not always possible to maintain this feeling of unity and oneness with the space around you, there are occasions when it might be valuable to cloak your energy field so that you can be more effective in your space clearing. Do not hesitate to protect yourself if you feel the need.

Steps to Take Prior to Using Protection Techniques

Before you do any protection techniques, follow these steps:

1. Set the intention that you are divinely protected from all that doesn't serve your highest purpose.

2. Say a prayer from the heart, for the highest good.

3. Activate general balance and harmony by staying grounded and connected with the earth's energy. You can do so through an activity such as the following:

- Allow roots to flow from you deep into Mother Earth.
- Walk on the earth.
- Touch a tree.

4. Stay connected with your higher power.

- Ask for assistance from God/Goddess/Creator/Great Spirit, guides, guardians, and angels, and humbly beseech guidance, assistance, and protection.

- Remember that divine energy is within you as well as around you and above you.

- Maintain a high vibration of gratitude, love, compassion, and joy. Like attracts like. Negative thoughts, feelings, and vibrations can deplete your energy. Do not suppress your emotions, however. Process all your emotions in a healthy manner and allow them to release so you can move forward with vibrant health and vitality.

- Be clear and full of light. Cleanse yourself as appropriate.

- Have a healthy respect for less than positive energies. However, do not allow yourself to come from a place of fear. Instead, come from a place of confidence, strength, and compassion. Ask for assistance when needed.

SPECIFIC PROTECTION TECHNIQUES

If you ever feel the need for extra protection, the following techniques are highly effective. These techniques are not specific to space clearing. You can do them anytime you feel you need an added barrier between you and the negative energy of the world.

You do not need to use all these techniques. However, you can try each of them, one at a time, to discover which work best for you. Alternatively, you might want to combine a few of them.

The best way to experiment with them is to try one during a non-space-clearing situation in which you are aware that you'll need your energy "mantle." For example, you can try a technique at a family gathering that always leaves you drained.

Technique 1: Spiral Visualization

Imagine two intertwined spirals like a DNA strand. They are twirling up from the earth like a whirlwind. Visualize yourself in the center.

Stomp twice—once with each foot—to activate the spirals. With each stomp, cry out "Haa!" with passion. (An interesting sidenote: in the Hawaiian language, the word *Haa* means both "breath" and "spirit.")

If you'd like to use colors in your visualization, make sure the entire whirlwind column of color is surrounded in shimmering, radiant white light. Visualize the colors as incredibly bright and sparkling. See "Colors for Protection" in Appendix A.

Technique 2: Breath of Fire

Breath of Fire is a powerful protecting and clearing kind of breath that has been done in Indian healing traditions for many hundreds of years. It clears your energy field and also creates a healing, protective energetic boundary around you. Breath of Fire is good for clearing your auric field after your space clearing as well.

1. Stand, if possible, allowing your pelvis and your body to be unrestricted so that energy can pump up from the earth and through your entire body.

2. Start with slow deep breaths through your nose and then increase the speed until you are doing a very rapid in-and-out breath. Allow your body to move naturally in alignment with your breathing.

3. Imagine that each breath is reinforcing your personal shield of energy around your body. (The visualization is very important for this technique.)

Technique 3: Talisman

You can use whatever feels powerful and protective to you as a talisman such as a crystal, stone, symbol, word, or special gift. The exact nature of the item is less important than the meaning that you assign to it.

Talismans can be worn around the neck or taped on the body. (If you use the latter method, use surgical tape or another tape that can be removed painlessly.) Consider taping your talisman onto the solar plexus area, which is where we lose energy. Notice that when people are afraid, they often wrap their arms over this area.

Make sure to cleanse your talisman periodically, via one of the methods in Part II. Also refer to the box "Simple Cleansing Techniques" on page 39.

If you'd like to use a stone as a talisman, refer to Appendix B for guidance in your selection. The following are particularly good options for protection; however, any stone that feels powerful and protective to you is a good one:

- Black tourmaline
- Iron pyrite
- Lingam

Note that a crystal, if used as a talisman, must be cleared immediately and reprogrammed. Be aware that a crystal can absorb energy rather than dispel it, if not used in a discerning way.

Technique 4: Salt

Salt can be carried in a pouch around the neck or in pockets during a clearing. Although the difference is subtle, rock salt is slightly more grounding than sea salt, but both are excellent—the less processed the better, and the bigger the crystals the better.

Consider taking a salt bath before and after a clearing. (Epsom salt can be used.) If done before, don't rinse off completely, ensuring there is a subtle mantle of salt on your body.

You can also take a shower and scrub with salt to create this mantle of energy. Make sure to use the salt under your armpits. Energetically your arms usually cover this area but when you lift your arms in your space clearing, it is exposed.

Technique 5: Angels and Spiritual Mentors

Call upon angels, guardian spirits, and spirits of the Four Elements to stand before you, behind you, and on either side of you, so that your spirit helpers surround and protect you. You can also call upon your ancestors for protection. This is powerful beyond measure.

Technique 6: Essential Oils

Spray or dab on protective essential oils, such as the following:

- Pine
- Fir
- Spruce
- Lemon
- Lime
- Grapefruit

- Bay Laurel
- Rosemary
- Juniper
- Frankincense
- Cardamom
- Rose oil

See Appendix D for more information on different essential oils.

Technique 7: Clothing Color

Even the clothing you wear can add some protective qualities. White is a reflective color and so adds some protection during a space clearing. For the qualities of other colors, see the box "Colors for Protection" in Appendix A.

Technique 8: The Power of Your Word

To deepen a protective mantle around you, declare out loud (or silently to yourself), "My word is law in my universe, and I am safe and strong no matter where I am." You can then thump the center of your chest three times with passion and say out loud, "I am safe!"

This can be done several times during a clearing if needed. Each time you hit your chest, say, "I am safe." Thumping the chest dispels anything that is not needed out of your energy field.

Technique 9: The Majesty of the Cross

Long before Christianity claimed it as its symbol, the Cross was a symbol of protection and sanctuary. Imagine a fine netting surrounding you that's made of thousands of crosses. You might imagine that the Creator (or Christ) is tossing this netting over you wherever you need protection.

Technique 10: Crystal Seal

1. Create or obtain a hand-drawn outline of your home.

2. In a meditative state, allow your fingers to lightly run over the map to sense which areas feel stuck or out of harmony. (This will help you later in your space clearing to determine where to spend the most time and energy.)

3. After noting these areas, take nine cleansed crystals and place eight in a circle around the map of the space . . . and one in the center of the space. "See" a circle of healing, protective energy surging into and sealing the area. Leave this in your home while you do this clearing. This creates a protective energy in the space while you are working there.

4. After you have done the clearing, take the drawing and burn it with the intent that the old energy has been replaced with new energy. Sprinkle the ashes outdoors.

5. Absolutely make sure that you cleanse the crystals before putting them away.

Technique 11: Tree of Light

1. Visualize yourself standing in the center of a trunk of a huge and very old, wise tree. (Old oak trees work well for this technique.)

2. Imagine the branches rising high above your head, reaching to the heavens and attracting vibrant energy. Visualize the massive roots from the tree going deep into the earth. Be aware of the grounding energy of the earth surging up through you.

3. Call upon the Spirit of the Tree to guard and protect you. Offer thanks for all the protection that is given.

4. Keep this visualization in mind as you do the space clearing. If you need to renew it periodically feel free to do so.

If you live in an area with some soulful trees, you might want to adopt one so that you not only have a Spirit Tree as your protector but also a physical tree that you can call upon. To adopt a tree, simply stand next to it in nature and imagine that you can communicate with it. Ask it if it is willing to be your protective tree. If it feels as if the tree is answering in the affirmative, then it will act as an energetic protector. (Most trees *love* to serve in this way. It's one of their gifts to humanity.)

Technique 12: Sphere of Divine Light

Immerse yourself in a sphere of divine white light, allowing it to flow through and surround you.

Alternatively, imagine yourself in an orb of pink light filled with pink etheric roses to represent unconditional love.

Technique 13: Light Shower

As you shower, imagine divine white light flowing over your body, cleansing your entire body and your energy fields . . . thus replenishing your energy and creating a sphere of light to protect you.

Technique 14: Mirror Bubble

Visualize yourself surrounded by a mirrored bubble with the reflective side facing out. Anything less than positive sent your way is cleansed and reflected back into the universe. You may wish to set the intention that anything serving your highest purpose is allowed to pass through, while anything else is reflected away.

Technique 15: Wall of Golden Light

Imagine a wall of golden light between you and whatever you wish to be protected from. Nothing can penetrate the wall of golden light.

PREPARING YOUR SPACE CLEARING TOOLS

Part II will delve into all the tools that you might choose for space clearing. It's important to note that the tools you use are only a vehicle for your intention and prayers. By themselves, they cannot sanctify a home. Your bell, drum, or gong only serves as a focal point for you to direct energy toward a space. However, the tools that you choose are important because when you feel a close connection to them, they serve to amplify your intention.

Choose Your Tools

Choosing a tool for space clearing is very individual. One person may fall in love with the frame drum and find that every time they hear its sound, they can sense energy more perceptively. Someone else may find that burning incense resins creates a powerful shift of consciousness in a space.

The best space clearing tool is the one that you feel most attracted to. How much you pay for it or where it came from does not matter as much as your love for it.

A tool that is loved will be a powerful ally in your quest to bring harmony into living spaces.

Empower and Attune Your Tools

Empower your space clearing tools before the first time you use them, and re-attune them before every space clearing. To do so, hold the tool close to your body and visualize it becoming an extension of your body and soul. When you and your space clearing instruments are thus attuned to each other, that bond creates a special kind of alchemy that strengthens with every space clearing ceremony that you perform. A tool that has been attuned to your energy is a powerful ally in your space clearing.

Name Your Tools

Naming your tools further facilitates their effectiveness. Naming is a powerful and magical act. In ancient cultures an instrument used for ceremonies was revered and named. Words structure reality and anytime you name something, you develop a much more intimate connection with it.

The feather fan I use for smudging is named "Dragon Wind." Every time I use it, I imagine that a powerful healing wind created by the wings of a magnificent emerald-green dragon is fanning the smoke into a room.

Before each use of a space clearing tool, mentally address it by its name. This will automatically call forth stronger, more resonant energy.

Cleanse Your Tools

Keep your space clearing tools scrupulously clean. Shake out or wash your altar cloth, incense burner, and other such items after each use. It's important to also energetically cleanse your tools before and after a space clearing. There are multiple methods described in Part II for doing so. Refer to the box "Simple Cleansing Techniques for your Tools" on page 39 for some good suggestions.

Properly Store Your Tools

Your space clearing tools should be held in a special place when not in use. Select a place that's clean and free of clutter—don't shove everything in a drawer or messy shelf. You may find it useful to wrap certain items in fabric. For example, wrapping your crystals in silk will help keep the energy intact. Use your intuition as to the qualities of different fabrics and colors, and see Appendix A for further guidance.

Simple Cleansing Techniques for Your Tools

1. *Sunlight:* Place the item in direct sunlight for three to four hours. (This is especially good for crystals.)

2. *Smoke:* Hold the item over smoldering incense, resins, herbs such as sage, or cedar needles. (This is a good method for cleansing your drums, bells, and feathers.)

3. *Prayers or chants:* Offer a prayer from the heart or chant a desired mantra until you feel the energy is cleansed. This is also a type of sound vibration.

4. *Sound vibration:* Gongs, singing bowls, and other musical instruments are wonderful for cleansing. See Chapter 6 for more details about their use.

5. *Fire:* Hold your tools above the flame of a small candle. Be sure not to hold them so close that they catch fire or become overheated. As you pass each tool through the fire's purifying energy, let your intention center on your purpose for the clearing and the part that the tool will play in it.

6. *Salt:* This method is excellent for clearing crystals. Cover the crystal completely in salt, or in at least 1 cup water with ½ cup salt, for at least 24 hours. Rock salt is slightly more grounding than sea salt, but both are excellent—the less processed the better, and the bigger the crystals the better.

7. *Oil:* Holding your item in your hand, rub eucalyptus oil over its entire surface. This is good for tools that are stone or metal. Other oils can be used; however, eucalyptus is especially cleansing. Begin at the base and work your way up to the top. (In the case of a crystal, for instance, you would start at the bottom or flat surface of the crystal and work up to the top facet, which is the tip or apex of the crystal where all sides come together.)

THE SACRED BLESSING ALTAR

The Blessing Altar creates a vortex of energy for the clearing. It grounds and stabilizes energy, allowing the space to adjust gently to the clearing so there isn't any ensuing chaotic energy. Furthermore, it magnifies your efforts during the clearing and activates spiritual guidance. It becomes a sacred center from which you can draw energy as you work throughout the home. It helps anchor and strengthen you during the space clearing.

In many ways the power of the altar lies in its visible appearance. The structure and objects of the altar appeal to our psyche because they give form to the formless and provide a visual representation of the Divine. It is difficult to comprehend the spiritual realm because of its unseeable nature. However, when objects are thoughtfully placed on an altar to physically represent thoughts, plans, ideas, or dreams—which by their very essence are invisible—this gives substance to your intentions. The care that goes into a Blessing Altar can positively impact an entire home.

Choose the Symbols for Your Blessing Altar

The first step in preparing your altar is to become clear about your intentions for the entire house. If you are doing a clearing for another, take care to interview them about their goals. Then, simply decide what altar objects would best symbolize those intentions.

Every object on the altar, as well as the placement of these objects, is meaningful. The organization of the altar creates a template for the rest of your ceremony, and the overall intention for your space clearing should be reflected in your Blessing Altar. Carefully chosen objects placed on your Blessing Altar in a deliberate and conscious way can create a mystic center of powerful energy that ripples in all directions.

The following is a list of some qualities commonly associated with a number of objects you might place upon your altar. It is by no means complete; this is intended only as a starting point.

Remember that symbols and their interpretations vary widely from culture to culture. Use what works for you; your intuition will be your true guide in your selection.

For ease of transport, I suggest keeping all your tools and altar cloths in a special basket or wooden box. (I like to call this the Blessing Basket.)

Your Altar Cloth

An altar cloth is the piece of fabric that will serve as your altar during your space clearing ceremony. You can go to a fabric store or specialty store to get cloths of all colors, materials, and designs to activate different kinds of energy.

Colors: Our response to light is very deeply ingrained in our nervous system. Because consciousness is so closely related to the spectrum of light, the color of your altar cloth and other items on your altar will dramatically affect the energy of your space clearing. See Appendix A for color associations you might want to consider.

Designs: Be aware of the symbolism in the designs that you choose. For example, I have an altar cloth with a serpent on it, which represents transformation and change. So if someone really wanted a new life, to let go of the old, this cloth might be a good fit. If you find life dull, you might reach for a colorful, sparkling cloth.

Fabrics: Note the fabric of your altar cloth. Every material has a different energy you can intuit. For example, a soft cashmere would be wonderful for someone who wanted to bring that soft, loving energy into his or her life.

You don't need to spend lots of money to get many different, expensive cloths; you can have just one altar cloth. Do not equate stuff with results.

Stones and Gemstones

Using specially chosen stones or metals on your Blessing Altar can quicken the specific kind of energy associated with them. See Appendix B for the qualities commonly associated with some gems and stones you may find useful.

Natural stones that you gather from special locations can be sources of healing energy for space clearing. Similarly, a stone given to you by a teacher or someone special to you will contain the energy of that connection. Placing these stones on your Blessing Altar is one way of implanting their energy in the space.

Plants and Other Offerings

On altars throughout the world, you will find offerings of fruit, flowers, and grains. These are traditionally used because they represent the bounty brought forth from the Earth Mother. A glowing orange, a small bowl of rice, a beautiful arrangement of bright flowers—all of these things add richness, beauty, and a feeling of abundance to the Blessing Altar, as well as anywhere else they are placed in the home. They call in these qualities for your clearing and can secure them into the energy of the home once your ceremony is complete.

When you are choosing items for your Blessing Altar, keep in mind the meaning that each item can bring to the overall energy of the home. An essential oil burner or a stick of incense can also deepen the energy of a clearing. (See Appendix D for guidance.) Turn to Appendix C for a list of the meanings of different flowers you might use to adorn your altar or use in a flower offering.

Here are a few other commonly used offerings and their meanings:

Fruits and Grains

- *Apple:* health, vitality
- *Corn:* harvest, abundance, fertility, blessing
- *Peach:* immortality, marriage, tenderness
- *Pomegranate:* fertility, unity of diversity
- *Mustard seed:* faith
- *Wheat:* abundance, harvest, intuition
- *Grains:* prosperity, renewal
- *Rice:* good fortune

Representations of the Four Elements

- *Air (feathers, "empty" bowl):* uplifting
- *Water (holy water):* cleansing and purifying
- *Fire (candles, incense):* transforming
- *Earth (sand, stones, or salt):* grounding

Other Offerings

- *Ashes:* purification, regeneration
- *Figurines of angels, holy deities, or totem animal allies:* calling forth spiritual assistance
- *Shells:* water, feminine energy, power of the sea and the moon
- *Wine:* blood of life, eternal life
- *Wreathes:* earth, cycle of life

Set Up Your Blessing Altar

Once you have decided which objects to use for your altar, in a deliberate, soulful way, set up your altar. You can set it on the floor, on a coffee table or table, or any place that feels central to the space that you are clearing. Take each item out of your Blessing Basket (or whatever you're using to contain them) in a ceremonial way with love and care.

You can do this arranging in silence, or you can say a blessing for each item on your Blessing Altar. For example, as you place an offering bowl filled with rice on your altar cloth, you might say:

I dedicate this offering of rice to abundance
and prosperity for this home.

Call for Spiritual Assistance at the Blessing Altar before the Space Clearing

After you have arranged the Blessing Altar, take a moment to center your thoughts. Hold the intention of what results you desire for the clearing. Then, either aloud or silently, offer prayers for the space and all who occupy the space. An example of a prayer might be:

I dedicate this space clearing to love, joy, and good health.
May harmony and peace embrace all the members of this family,
and may all who enter this place find comfort here. I humbly
ask for spiritual guidance during this clearing.

Beginnings are important, and the initiation of any space clearing is a sacred time. If you start clearing a house or office without first taking the proper steps, your ceremonies will not be as profound and powerful as they could have been. Your Blessing Altar is the place where you begin your ritual, open your heart, and call for spiritual guidance. Angels, spirit guides and guardians, ancestors, and totem allies respond and send beneficial healing energy when prayers are sent straight from the heart.

Integrate Energy Following the Space Clearing— the Completion Blessing Ceremony

The completion ceremony performed at the Blessing Altar is as significant as the one done at the beginning. The time and energy you spend at the end of the ceremony will integrate the energy of the space clearing you have just performed. If a space clearing is done without grounding and integration, then disruption and turmoil can occur afterward.

The length of time that a completion blessing ceremony takes may vary. Usually it lasts about 10 minutes, but it may last longer depending on individual needs.

The process itself is very simple. Spend as much time as you intuitively feel is necessary at your Blessing Altar, serenely sending forth prayers for the home and its occupants. The following is an example of a prayer you might say at the conclusion of your clearing:

Creator, spiritual guardians, and angels, thank you for the loving assistance that was given to us during this space clearing. Thank you for the peace and joy that is now flowing into this home. May the benefits of this clearing and blessing continue for the months ahead. May the wonderful positive energy that has been instilled in this home bring comfort and rejuvenation to all.

Space clearing without integration can be compared to the process of continually stirring up a stagnant pond: the water will appear disrupted and murky. Space clearing can stir up old energy, and it can make an environment feel disturbed and agitated afterward. However, when energy is integrated at the conclusion of a space clearing, churned-up energy in the home is smoothed into gentle, flowing energy. It becomes like a stream of fresh water gently flowing into a stagnant pond, which eventually turns clear, without turmoil. Similarly, a grounded space clearing creates clarity and harmony throughout the home without undue disruption.

The completion ceremony done at the Blessing Altar grounds the energy of the home and prevents a sense of upheaval afterward.

Without this integration, it is not uncommon for repressed energy to rise to the surface.

For example, if a couple is harboring suppressed, festering anger or resentment toward each other, space clearing can result in turmoil and even loud arguments after the clearing, unless there is a grounding. The couple might state, "Before the clearing everything was peaceful, but now there is chaos!" What they called "peaceful" might be very stagnant, suppressed emotions, but they usually don't take kindly to you pointing that out to them.

Space clearing removes stagnant energy, which may be like allowing suppressed negative energy to rise to the surface. This can be like lancing a boil. Old issues can rise to the surface after an ungrounded space clearing. However, when there is an integration ceremony at the Blessing Altar, a home will be filled with clearer, more balanced energy. This way, hidden issues can rise to the surface in a safer and more harmonious manner, rather than through upheaval.

A space clearing done without integration can sometimes also cause problems in the house itself, such as water pipes breaking or fuses blowing out. To avoid emotional or physical disruptions after a space clearing, please be sure to follow the steps and suggestions in this chapter with clear focus and an open mind and heart.

CHAPTER 4

Clutter Clearing

is

Modern-Day Alchemy

As a stand-alone practice space clearing is immensely valuable; however, when space clearing is done in conjunction with clutter clearing, the results are much more powerful. To fully transform your living spaces with space clearing, consider also doing some clutter clearing.

In order to understand the deeper forces at play regarding clutter and why clearing it is such an excellent complement to your space clearing, it's essential to look at the energy in our homes and realize how it affects us. True clutter clearing is a kind of alchemy that can transform every aspect of life. But in order to activate this alchemy, we must understand how we are influenced by the frequencies and energies of the objects in our homes and why clutter clearing can be a spiritual pursuit.

What many do not realize is that the energy in your home and the objects you surround yourself with profoundly affect the energy you radiate into the world. Your "stuff" can produce a remarkably negative (or positive) influence on the way you feel and on every aspect of your life. When you surround yourself with objects filled with love and happiness, the energy in your home or office will lift you up. That positive vibration stays with you even outside of this space.

It's important to note that simply clearing the things you don't love and don't use is not enough. You need to get to the source of what your personal clutter truly represents. For example, if your clutter represents your fear of not having or being enough, then just getting rid of your stuff will not solve the problem, and it will likely accumulate again. Once you understand your inner blockages, you can clear them at the source. You can step beyond that fear, acknowledging that you have enough and that you *are* enough. Once you gain the faith and the confidence to believe that all is well, you can remove the energetic wall between you and your potential.

The ultimate goal at the end of this process is not just a more organized and clean home, but a sense of having room to breathe, the ability to move more freely through each day, and the feeling of being more vibrant and empowered in every area of life. Clutter clearing is so much more than cleaning or organizing, it is the alchemy of life. It can help you heal and empower your life in wonderful ways.

WHAT IS CLUTTER?

Clutter is an accumulation of things that are no longer needed or loved. The following are all examples of clutter in its simplest definition:

- Any object that you don't love or use
- Half-finished and never-started projects
- Anything that has been broken for a long time or that has parts missing
- Clothes that don't fit or that you don't like
- Too many objects or pieces of furniture for the size of the space
- Old letters, photos, coupons, etc., that do not bring you joy

From a spiritual perspective, however, letting go of physical "stuff" equates with letting go of blockages and barriers in your life. This is because clutter—whether it's physical or emotional—is never just about the stuff; it's a signpost that indicates other things going on in your life beneath the surface. The following are all examples of clutter from this perspective:

- A buffer in regard to life (such as fear of being "seen" or fear of being rejected or judged)
- Something to fill an emotional hole remaining from childhood issues that have gone unaddressed
- An external symbol of being enough when you don't internally feel like enough

- A family pattern (healthy or unhealthy)
- A feeling of security or safety
- An outward distraction from looking within and focusing on self-care
- An attempt to hold on to old relationships, experiences, or situations, even if they no longer serve you

COMMON REASONS PEOPLE COLLECT CLUTTER

So why do we keep clutter? Often, the root cause is fear. For example, we might worry about needing a particular item in the future and being unable to replace it. By thinking this way, you create your own need and stop trusting that the universe will provide for you. This belief becomes self-perpetuating, because fear of the future tends to create a fearful future.

If you believe all your needs will be met in the future, they usually will be. What you expect in life often becomes reality. A person who expects to have a bad day is usually not disappointed, while someone anticipating a good day is usually rewarded. If you are holding on to junk because you are fearful about the future, get rid of it! Trust that you will be exactly where you need to be in the future. No matter what your reason for keeping clutter, it clogs the energy in your home, your body, and your life.

The following are the most common reasons—not all of which are bad—that we keep clutter:

- It makes you feel safe and gives you a sense of security. (A year of stored food can give us the feeling that we are secure in times of scarcity.)
- It makes you feel validated and gives you a sense of self-worth. (The trophy you won in weightlifting or the service award you gained at work can contribute to a feeling of self-worth.)

- It anchors you to your past. (Clutter can contribute to a sense of continuum regarding your family and friends. It can have sentimental significance.)

- It provides comfort. (There's something comforting about being surrounded by things that you've had for a long time.)

- It acts as an affirmation of being loved. (The painting your ex-husband gave you might be an affirmation that there was a time when love flowed between you both.)

- It affirms the identity of whom you desire to be. (The cross-country skis that you've never used, the flamboyant red scarf, or the colorful hair attachments that are still in their box could all be reminders of the wild and free person that you desire to be in the future.)

- It gives you the feeling that you are working on self-improvement. (Just looking at those self-help books makes you feel spiritual, even though you've never read them.)

- It feels like a duty. (The family heirlooms or gifts from friends carry with them a sense of guilt. You may worry about the anger of other family members or the friend who gave the items to you because you didn't keep them.)

- It gives you a sense of the familiar and routine. (This can be reassuring, but sometimes it works against you. For example, some people stay in abusive relationships or low-paying jobs, or continue addictive behaviors, simply because they are familiar territories.)

—— **EXERCISE** ——

Clear One Thing with Intention

Anytime you need a little lift in life, consider a small session of clutter clearing. If you have been feeling sluggish, uninspired, or overwhelmed, then this is an excellent time to do some clearing. Even the simplest act will have a positive effect on how you feel if it is done with the intent of transforming the energy in your life and the energy you give off.

Preparation

Even if you intend to clear only one object, it is important to take some time for preparation. This will dictate how powerful the transformation will be from any clearing that you do.

You do not need to go through all the steps of Stage 1 as you would for a full space clearing. Your preparation might simply be cleansing, such as taking a shower or a bath, before you clear the object. It might be lighting a candle with a prayer. It can even be a short blessing such as, "May Higher Wisdom be with me as I clear this object with intention."

Intuition

Your intuition is crucial in sensing the energy of an object while you clear clutter. When you have quieted your thoughts, visualize one of the objects in your home that you are considering letting go of. Imagine connecting with the consciousness of the object. Tune in to it. Sense the deeper energies within it. Does it carry the energy of people who might have owned it before you? Does it seem to hold the emotions of the place it was created or the people who made it? Does it have a message for you? Does it desire to stay in your environment, or is it ready to travel onward? Use your imagination . . . and trust what it reveals to you.

Intention

Clearing clutter involves doing so with intention. Simply throwing things away or donating them to a charity won't necessarily change or heal your life. However, when you release items with the intention that something changes in life, so it shall. The following questions will help hone your intention for clearing the one object you choose for this exercise.

Take a moment to close your eyes so you can get clear on each answer. You won't have time to practice this process with every object when you're doing a major clutter clear. However, by taking the time to do so now with a single object, you train your intuition and increase your understanding of how the process works.

- What is the one object I want to clear?
- Do I use it? Do I love it?
- How does this object make me feel?
- Where does it reside in my home? Would it feel better/ worse in another area of my home? (Sometimes clutter in one place would not be clutter in another place.)
- How important is this object to me?
- How will I feel if this object is not in my life?
- How will I feel if I keep it?
- Am I ready to release this object? If not now, when?
- What do I desire in my life as a result of releasing this object?

After choosing your item with intention and answering these questions, stand in silence. Visualize the positive outcome now and in the future. Affirm the positive outcome.

Consider writing your answers down. You may begin to detect a pattern with the answers to many of your objects. Record anything you feel happens as a result of your experience. It will be beneficial to see your growth in just a few weeks of releasing things from your life that you don't love or use.

HONORING CLUTTER THAT'S DIFFICULT TO RELEASE

Honor the things that you clear from your home, and honor the things that you decide to keep. By doing this, you'll maintain your energy and open your life to beautiful possibilities.

One way of releasing your attachment to your clutter is by talking to the objects and communicating gratitude: "Thank you for being in my life." After expressing thanks for the joy, meaning, or learning that this object has given in your life, you can then release it with grace.

Another way to honor objects you'd like to let go of is by taking photos of the objects. This is a wonderful option for things like mementos, gifts, or heirlooms that you don't really want to let go of, but don't have the space for. You can create an album or collage, whether physical or digital, so you can connect with the objects whenever you like.

You can also journal about cherished objects. Write the story of how they came into your life, how they made you feel, and how much you appreciated them at one point. Write out any old memories associated with them. Give them life through your words, and then let them move on with their journey.

CLEARING BASICS

Now you're ready to start clutter clearing! To do so, you'll need five boxes designated in the following ways:

- *The Throwaway Box:* This is for items that have done their service and would not be used by someone else.

- *The Giveaway Box:* Use this for items that still have a life and purpose for someone else.

- *The Recycle Box:* In this box, collect items to be released that can be recycled.

- *The Maybe Later/Store Box:* Use this for items that you are unsure about or not quite ready to release. These are items that you don't use but still have an attachment to. (Often, guilt or fear is why we keep a thing that we don't love.) When the clearing session is complete, these items will be stored separately. Seal the box and mark it with a date—either today's date as a reminder, or a future date upon which you will give the box away if you haven't needed anything from it.

- *The Keep Box:* This is for items that will be kept, and during the second half of the clutter clearing session will be stored or arranged appropriately.

Depending on your personality, you may want to add the following boxes as part of your sorting process:

- *Free Box:* This is for items to donate to a cause, or just place outside your home with a free sign (if you live in a populated area where this is allowed).

- *Gift Box:* You can use this for items that you can gift to other people. However, don't burden others with stuff for the sake of making you feel better. This should only be used for gifts that will be truly appreciated by the receivers.

- *Find Alternatives Box:* This is a box for objects with a monetary value. You might sell these items online or to a consignment shop, or dismantle and repurpose certain objects for another project.

Set Goals

The next step is to set some reasonable goals. Attempting to categorize everything in a room may get a little overwhelming, both physically and emotionally. I suggest clearing one small area at a time. Go drawer by drawer, or wall by wall. While some folks prefer to empty the entire closet, clean it until it sparkles and only put back items they use and love, this approach can be too extreme for others.

For most, clutter clearing is not an activity that happens all in one day. You may get through a bedroom or closet in one day, but even that may be too emotionally exhausting for you. Clutter clearing should be a healing process, not an overwhelming task that you dread each time you clear a space. Take your time, be thoughtful, and make sure that love and sacred intent goes into every movement during your clutter clearing sessions.

Part of setting your goals is to figure out how much time you have to clear. Once you figure out what to clear, set a timer for half the time you have. You will empty and clear until that timer goes off. For the rest of the time, you will clean, organize, and put things away.

Tap Into the Energy of Your Space

After you've set all these logistics, it's time to tap into the energy of your space. Ask yourself these questions each time you start a new room:

- How do I feel when I am in this room?
- How would I like to feel in this space?
- What is the current function or use of this room?
- What is the ideal function or use of this space?
- In relation to the other spaces in my home, how important is this room to me?

- How would I like to feel when I am done clearing things associated with this issue?

- What is the current function of this issue in my life?

- What is ideal for this issue in my life?

- In relation to the other issues in my life, how important is this issue to me?

The way you answer these questions will help guide you as you clear.

ROOM ORDER FOR CLEARING CLUTTER

From a feng shui perspective, clutter can affect your fortunes and every aspect of your life. Clutter in your kitchen can affect your finances. Clutter in the bedroom can affect your love relationships. Clutter in hallways can affect your arteries. Clutter on a spiral staircase can affect your heart. Clutter in a basement affects your ability to be grounded. Clutter in an attic can mean that problems hang over your head in life, and so on.

The following list may be helpful as you prepare for your clutter clearing. Here is an order of the rooms to consider clearing first:

1. Bedroom (master)
2. Closet (master bedroom)
3. Bathroom (master)
4. Kitchen
5. Other bedrooms (and closets)
6. Other bathrooms
7. Dining room
8. Living room
9. Front entry
10. Basement
11. Attic
12. Hallways and stairs
13. Garage
14. Car

—— **EXERCISE** ——

Clutter Assessment for Each Room

Sit quietly, close your eyes, and imagine your home. Scan it in your mind's eye, then choose a room that you feel needs to be cleared.

Visualize yourself in the room. What are you most aware of? What captures your attention? Are there objects that make you smile, or that you enjoy being around? Are there objects that you may prefer to pass over, or that make you sad, or that trigger uneasy feelings such as guilt? Use the questions below to help you understand your feelings about those objects. This process can also allow you to see if you are ready to release an object from your life. Notice any items that might need to be released. Select your top three.

Visualize item number one. Ask yourself:

- How does it make me feel?
- Do I love it?
- Do I need it?
- Is it something I want to release?
- What would I need to do to let go of it?

For instance, maybe you are imagining an old vase that was handed down to you from your beloved grandmother. It does not match the room, you never use it, but you would feel guilty if you let it go. Maybe it would help if you took a picture of it, journaled about the memories you have of your grandmother, and documented having the vase. That might help relieve those feeling of guilt or fear that you are losing a piece of your past, if you were to release the vase.

Remember, the vase is not your grandmother, and your grandmother would never want her gift to you to hold you back or cause you grief. She would, most likely, want you to let it go and open yourself to the opportunity to grow!

Ask yourself the same questions for items two and three, writing down your answers in a journal if you feel called to do so.

BEGIN THE CLUTTER CLEARING

We are now ready to begin clutter clearing!

Figure out how much time you are going to clear, then set the timer for half that amount of time. For the first half of time, you'll clear. During the second half, you'll organize and put things away.

Then, start clearing. As you pick up each item, ask yourself:

- Do I love it?

- Do I use it?

- Do I really need this?

- Does this fit who I am? Does this fit who I desire to be in the future?

- Does this make my energy go up or down, or remain neutral?

- Why am I keeping this? Who am I keeping this for?

- What will my life be like if I let it go?

- Will the freedom I gain by getting rid of this outweigh any possible regrets I may have by getting rid of it?

If the answer is *yes* for the first couple of questions, then the object automatically goes in the Keep Box.

If you're having a hard time figuring out what box to put something in, sit with your feelings of discomfort. Remember that clutter in one place may not be clutter in another. Perhaps an item feels like clutter simply because it's in the wrong place. Each item in your home needs its own specific place to live. When all are in their perfect place, they feel uplifting rather than like clutter.

CHAPTER 5

The Energy of Your Home, Room by Room

Cultures throughout the world and throughout time, have arranged items in their homes to maximize the feeling and the energy within. In Asia this tradition is called *feng shui*, but it has many names and numerous forms throughout the world. The art of feng shui is also called the art of placement, because the placement of the objects in your home can influence the way you feel and even your life circumstances. Although the details differ from culture to culture, the overall beliefs, method, and end results are very similar. By having the ability to listen to your home, feng shui techniques can help you design the objects in your home to allow you to work through blockages and clear negative energy. This practice will also help you learn to understand the deeper meaning of your home. When you have cleared clutter and attended to the feng shui of your home, you space clearing will be even more potent.

Understanding a bit about the feng shui of your home will help you better understand about the space clearing you do there. The first step in learning about feng shui is the understanding that you already have an intuitive sense about what feels good in your home. You don't necessarily need to hire an expert. Here is a simple rule to help you understand the feng shui of your home:

If it feels good, it's good feng shui.
If it feels bad, it's bad feng shui.

But just to give you a little additional help, here are a few basics to enable you to get oriented with the overall position of your home and its surroundings, as well as each room, so that you can understand why a room might feel the way is does.

FENG SHUI AND ENERGY

The directions play an important role in feng shui. Ancient Chinese masters understood the power of the hidden forces flowing from each direction, which are emphasized in the ancient perspective of the Asian Compass School of feng shui. In this tradition, the directions of the compass—called *lo pan*—are used for many deliberations and decisions.

Like some Native Americans, feng shui masters assigned a mythical creature to each direction as a connector to the power of that direction. You can use these associations when you think about your home and how the different energies of each direction affect it.

- *East, the dragon:* beneficial, creative powers
- *South, the phoenix:* expansive, joyful energy
- *West, the tiger:* unpredictable, transforming power
- *North, the tortoise:* wise, enduring strength

Note: The following qualities for north and south are associated with the Northern Hemisphere. Therefore, reverse them if you live in the Southern Hemisphere. The east and west meanings stay the same.

East

Space clearing in the eastern part of your home invites new and vibrant opportunities to come into your life.

The qualities associated with the power of the east are derived from the fact that this is the direction of the rising sun. For this reason, new beginnings are commonly associated with this direction. The Spirit of the East is aligned with the power of springtime. Spring is the season of awakening after the darkness and dormancy of winter. In Vastu—the type of feng shui of India—it's thought to be beneficial to have one's front door face the east. East is the home of dawn and symbolizes the waxing of the new moon. Freshly planted seeds, shoots pushing their way up through the soil, eggs waiting to hatch in a nest, and newborn babies are all events linked with the east. It's a time of growth, renewal, and vibrancy. The east is a place of hopes, dreams, and new plans.

Words associated with east: activation, inspiration, optimism, striving, growth, vigor, enlightenment

South

Space clearing in the southern portion of a home invites expansion of your projects and relationships, and growth in your business.

The power of the south lies in expansion and rapid growth. It is the home of summer, the midday sun, and the full moon. Crops are tall. Days are warm. The south is associated with the rapid growth of childhood. The idea that is born in the east is now nurtured and strengthened in the south.

Words associated with south: expansion, nurture, trust, abundance, energy, fruitfulness, activity, passion, exuberance, vitality

West

Space clearing in the western portion of a home opens you up to the completion of lingering projects and the release of old, limiting patterns regarding self-awareness, relationships, career, and finances.

In the cycle of life, the west is the realm of autumn, the setting sun; it symbolizes the energy of the waning moon. Crops are harvested. Leaves fall from trees. The west is associated with the years of change, maturation, discovery, transformation, experimentation, and completion. It is the time when childhood has been surrendered and adulthood has emerged. The idea or the project that was born in the east and nurtured in the south is now tried out and revised in the west. Cycles of experimentation move toward completion.

Words associated with west: completion, transformation, harvest, change, transition, surrender, release, purification, withdrawal

North

Space clearing in the northern portion of a home encourages your life to become grounded. Powerful insights emerge within you, and your connection to the Creator increases.

North is the realm of winter, the longest night, and the dark of the moon. North is associated with introspection, the achievement of maturity, and the wisdom of elders. It is also the realm of death and rebirth.

Words associated with north: consolidation, introspection, tranquility, meditation, retreat, rest, renewal, dormancy, inner guidance, incubation, wisdom, reflection

Center

Space clearing in the center of your home encourages your life to become more centered, calm, and balanced.

The center is the place where the many become one—where the separate parts of the self come together to become whole. The center is the heart of harmony and the Spirit of the Home. It is the place of healing where fragmentation is magically transformed into integration and unity.

Words associated with center: focus, spirit, awareness, intuition, unity, oneness

Flowing from each direction is a powerful force that is constantly affecting the flow of energy in your home. To discover the influences of the directions on your home, try the following exercise.

——— EXERCISE ———

The Directions and Influence on Your Home Energy

Step 1: Draw the outline shape of your home from an eagle's view, as if you were looking down on it from above. This will be similar to blueprints or a floor plan of your home.

Step 2: Use a compass to determine the directions in relation to your home. Label each direction on the drawing of your home.

For example, if the front of your home has a garage door, front door, and living-room window facing east, then write the word *East* along the front of your house drawing. This will give you a visual of how the directional energy is coming into your home.

Step 3: Next, draw the outline shape again and add surrounding buildings, vegetation, and land masses to show where your house sits in relation to the surrounding landscape. Notice how any of these factors may be affecting the flow of directional energy into your home.

To take our previous example, if there is a large obstruction on the front of your home, it could be blocking the east's creative energy from entering. To help diminish this blocking effect, you may need to activate the energy of the east.

Step 4: To activate the energy of a space in your home, start by clutter clearing. To use our example, you would want to focus on clearing clutter from the front door area and living room with the east-facing window. Then do a space clearing ceremony.

Next, you can increase the life-force energy in this space with something alive, like a houseplant. You might also choose a symbolic object that represents creativity, such as a painting of spring—the season that is associated with east—and hang it by the front door. Placing something here that represents dawn or new beginnings would activate the energy of the east too.

Another way to stimulate the energy of a particular direction is to cultivate the part of your garden that lies on this side of your home. Planting flowers, bushes, or trees on the eastern side can instantly enhance the east's energy of rebirth.

THE BEDROOM: SANCTUARY FOR THE SOUL

The master bedroom is generally where you spend the most hours of your day and is considered the most important room in the house. It is the first thing you see when you wake up in the morning; it is where you go to rest and rejuvenate; it is where you go to heal when you are sick. The bedroom is the start of each new day and the start of new life (as the place where many babies are conceived). It is the place where you deepen your relationship, and where dreams are hatched.

When you space clear your bedroom, it can affirm excellent, intimate relationships; it can help you become renewed, rested, and nurtured in life; and it can support creative insights springing forth during your dreams.

The first thing you see each morning when you awake, and the last thing you see each night when you go to bed, can set a metaphoric energy for your day and for your nocturnal hours. Ask, "If the first thing I see in the morning (and before bed) said something about my life, what might it be?"

What you see when you first wake up can influence your entire day. If the first thing you see in the morning is clutter and chaos, this activates energy of chaotic disorganization in your life. But if the first thing you see is a meditating Buddha or a vase of fresh flowers, you activate peaceful, beautiful energy in your life.

THE CLOSET: YOUR IDENTITY

Naturally, the second most important room in the house to clear is the space attached to the master bedroom—the master closet. Our clothes represent our identity, how we feel about ourselves, and how we present ourselves to the world.

Clothes hold energy, which is why it is important to cleanse and clear any that we purchase. Secondhand clothing holds the residual energy of those it was worn by. Even new clothing holds the energy of those who made it and those who worked at the shop where you purchased it. To clear clothing, you can do a thorough washing with intention, then hang the item in the sun for a few hours, or simply spritz it with essential oils. (See the box "Simple Cleansing Techniques" on page 39.)

Honor each article of clothing in your closet. Fold it with love, and thank it for being in your life. Thank it for protecting you from the elements. Thank it for making you feel confident and sexy or for making you feel warm and comfortable. Declare out loud that you appreciate it.

Remember that every intention will stay with that item as a blessing for the next time you use it. Fill your clothes with love and purpose, and you will be blessed with love and purpose the next time you wear them.

THE BATHROOM: THE OASIS

After the master bedroom and closet have been cleared, the next most important room in the house is the master bathroom. The bathroom's underlying energy should be cleansing and purifying. It is a place of potential deep relaxation, and the place in which you adorn yourself. It's an intimate space where you should not feel vulnerable, anxious, or overwhelmed. In this space you should feel comfortable, loved, and replenished. It is the place where you can wash away and/or release that which you do not need.

THE FRONT DOOR: ENTRANCE

Your front door is an intersection between your outer life and your inner life. In feng shui, it's called the "mouth of energy," meaning that it is where beneficial energy can enter your home, the way food enters your body. The energy of your entrance can make a powerful difference in the quality of your life. It sets a frequency and tone that can influence you in the deepest ways.

The front door is considered the face of your home. Just like you "put your face on" so you can greet people and face the world each day, make sure your home has its best face on. Make it a beautiful, vibrant, and welcoming place. It is very important to allow for your front door to open freely, without noise or creaking, and without obstruction of furniture or objects. This is the entrance to your home, and good energy should be welcome to flow freely from the outside in.

THE KITCHEN AND DINING AREA: ABUNDANCE

Your kitchen is the heart of your home, representing all that nourishes and nurtures you. It is a place for family gatherings, deep conversations, and decision-making. It is where your stomach and your soul are fed. It is where secrets are shared, and holidays are celebrated. It symbolizes the place of ancient tribal meetings and family get-togethers. It's an important room to help create a cohesive family energy. A space-cleared, clutter-free kitchen helps activate excellent health.

The dining areas and table should be considered a sacred space in your home. It holds a penultimate role in family dynamics. Your dining area might be attached to your kitchen or it might be a separate room or area. Wherever it is, it symbolizes the gathering place for friends and family. The deeper energy of the dining area supports wonderful and loving relationships when it is cleared and clean, even relationships with people that never enter your home. That is how powerful this energy is.

The table should be clear of clutter so you can eat and enjoy the company of the family together, without obstructions or emotional triggers in the way (a project that is behind schedule strewn across the table, for instance). Find a new place to store the mail or the paperwork that gets dropped off on the dining table. Create another place for the work project that covers the table. Honor this dining table as the symbolic space to nurture your body, your soul, and your relationships.

THE LIVING ROOM: SANCTUARY OF JOY

Each space of our home fulfills a different aspect of life. The living room should be a sanctuary for gatherings, a place you can unwind and relax. It should support pleasant conversations and entertainment.

What is the underlying energy of your living room? What is the overall feeling? Is it dark or is it light? Is there room to breathe, to relax, to wind down from the pressures of the day?

If you want new opportunities, a new relationship, or fresh new energy to flood your life, this is where you can start to make the space for it.

THE HOME OFFICE: EXCELLENCE

Does your energy drop (and your heart sink) when you enter your home office? Do you instantly feel there is too much to do and not enough time to accomplish it all?

Or do you enter your home office with a feeling of excitement and enthusiasm about what can be achieved? Does your heart sing just upon entering this space?

You want to be able to look at your home office and be excited to work. Everything in your home office should help you produce excellence and propel you toward productivity. It should be a place that gives you joy. The energy of your home office influences all the work that you do there. You want to feel at ease here while you go about your business.

THE ATTIC AND BASEMENT: THE PAST AND THINGS HIDDEN

The attic and basement are typically the seasonal storage space and the home for things from the past. They can represent things that are hidden from sight in life or things that are repressed within us.

The energy of your attic can make you feel like things are looming overhead. It can feel like there is a heavy weight hanging over you.

Your basement represents things that lie beneath the surface, such as things from your past, and issues within your life that you have been carrying with you for a long time. The basement is also your foundation. The energy in the basement can make you feel like you are stagnant and can't move forward or like you are stuck in one place in life. As you clear this area, affirm, "My foundations are strong. All that needs to surface is surfacing in my life. I do not repress things in my life. I am open, clear, and free."

If you wish to focus on clearing the past, spend time nurturing the basement, clearing clutter and clearing the space, filling it with love, cleaning with intent, lighting and decorating to balance the energy, and placing the items you love and need in their new home with a purpose.

THE GARAGE: WELCOME

The garage is often the last thing someone sees when they leave for the day and the first thing they see when they return. It sets the tone for the beginning and the end of the day. The energy from the garage can be so strong that it can filter into the rooms that surround and are connected to the garage.

When you leave and return to your home, you want the space to feel open rather than oppressive. Place something of welcoming beauty where you can see it when you pull into the garage; it will uplift your energy every time you come home.

The time and energy that you spend implementing changes in your home will magnify a positive healing energy in your life tenfold. Sometimes it happens in magical and mysterious ways. The more you clear the space in your home, the more inner space is revealed in your soul.

PART II

The

Deeper Energy

of Your

Space Clearing

Tools

CHAPTER 6

Sound— *the* Power *of* Vibrational Energy

Your space clearing can be magnified through the power of sound. Sound has the ability to mystically restore harmony in objects, people, and environments. The results obtained are real and lasting. For this reason, sound has been highly valued for space clearing for thousands of years. In ancient cultures, sound was traditionally used to shift energy and to allow access to altered states of consciousness. In monasteries and temples throughout history, sacred sound has been used to create hallowed ground. Healers, shamans, priestesses, and priests have used sound for healing, purification, and blessing rituals. You can use these same techniques to harmonize your home; however, it is valuable to first gain an understanding of the spiritual nature of sound.

An early creation myth of our planet states that all life began with primordial sound. As the sound spiraled round and round, it combined with matter to create the varying forms of animate and inanimate life on Earth, and each form was imbued with its own sound. These ancient beliefs are consistent with the principles of modern physics, which state that all atoms and molecules are in a constant state of movement, thus creating a resonance that can be described as a kind of sound vibration. It's as if each atom is singing its own unique song, which combines with the sounds of other atoms to create a collective harmonic.

When shamans speak of the "song of the grasses," they are referring to the fact that they can actually perceive the silent—but very real—harmonic vibration created in nature. They understand that there are two aspects of sound: audible sound and silent sound. Audible sound can touch our emotions and even create a physical vibration that can shatter glass. However, the most powerful sounds are those that you don't hear. These can also be some of the most beautiful. Both audible and silent sounds are used in space clearing.

The energy of both of these kinds of sound surrounds you continuously. Sound is vibration and each flower, stone, and river—in fact, every single thing around us—has its own vibration. Even human-made objects have their own sound. The oak dresser, the antique rug, and the glass vase all have their unique sound vibrations. And when the vibration of a person, place, or thing is out of synchronization with its own innate rhythm, the result is discord. When sound is used as a space clearing tool, it can bring everything in a room back into harmony.

If you ring a bell or clap in a room that is out of balance, the sound will seem dull and muffled. After the negative energy of the room has been cleared, you can hear the difference; sounds will be crisper, sharper, and much clearer. When you use a musical instrument to cleanse the energy of an environment, the sounds created actually "tune" every board, brick, wall, and object within that environment.

Sound creates geometric forms. Photographs taken of fine powder placed on a membrane while varying sounds are played show the powder arranging itself into beautiful mandala-like formations and symbols. Changes in pitch and tone even cause some patterns to spiral in geometric configurations, resembling the images seen in a kaleidoscope, precise and dramatic. The sounds created in space clearing utilize the energy imprints of these shapes, orchestrating a kind of synchronization and resonance that attunes the entire area.

CLEARING A ROOM USING SOUND

Drums, rattles, gongs, bells, chimes, wooden click sticks, and tingsha cymbals have traditionally been used for space clearing. However, any musical instrument can be effective in space clearing. In fact, your own voice, the clapping of your hands, a rain stick, a simple reed flute, or an instrument you have made yourself can all be used. The single most important consideration is the personal connection you feel to the instrument you have chosen. A tool that is loved will emanate a strong and vibrant energy. A tool that means nothing to you or one that is treated carelessly will not be as effective, no matter how much it cost or where it came from.

Sound alone cannot harmonize the energy in a room. It is the magical outcome of sound empowered by your intention that creates a miraculous shift of energy. Effective space clearing happens only when your heart is open and your intention is clear ... only then can you effectively project energy through your tool.

Before your clearing, hold your instrument close to you and imagine your energy merging with its spirit. Enter into the realm where you are not separate from the tool—where it becomes a part of you. As you create a sound, shift your consciousness so you can feel it resonate inside of you. Imagine sound radiating out from you to fill the room, tuning each and every corner and object in the room. You are the conductor and every object in the room is being harmonized under your direction.

When using sound, it can be helpful to employ a range of sizes of the same instrument. For example, if you are using bells, you can begin with a large bell to break up the heavy, stagnant energy, and then move to a small bell to refine and distill fresh new energy. You might circle the room once with the larger bell and then again with the higher pitched bell.

CLEARING INDIVIDUALS USING SOUND

Shamans have used sound for balancing and healing people's energy fields since prehistoric times. After you have cleared the energy of a home or office using sound, it is valuable to also attune the energy of the people who will be using the space. This aligns their energy with the newly cleared space. This can be done with the individual in a sitting, standing, or lying down position, depending on the personal preferences and comfort concerns of the person being cleared.

To clear a person's energy using sound, take your bell, singing bowl, gong, drum, tuning fork, or other sound instrument and create sounds as you move the instrument up and down the body. *Important:* Make sure no loud sounds are made next to the ears, as this can be uncomfortable. As you work, listen carefully to the sounds you are making. If you find any place where the sound seems more muffled or where you sense that energy is stuck, continue to concentrate sound in that area of the body until you feel the energy shift.

If the person is lying down, you can magnify the effect of the sound by positioning stones or gems on the body in relation to the seven chakras of the body. Early Sanskrit texts speak of chakras as spinning wheels of energy at various points in the body. Each energy point correlates with a different aspect of life. (See Appendix B for guidance on specific stones to choose.)

Place stones in the following areas:

- *1st chakra:* near the base of spine, or on the pubic bone
- *2nd chakra:* on the center of the abdomen
- *3rd chakra:* on the diaphragm area
- *4th chakra:* on the center of the chest
- *5th chakra:* on the throat
- *6th chakra:* on the center of the forehead
- *7th chakra:* on the floor/bed above the head

You can also lay stones, shells, or flowers in a ring around the person to create a circle of protective and healing energy. This will enhance the energy created by the sound work you are doing.

BELLS

Bells have the ability to shatter accumulated stagnant energy by producing a sound that permeates the molecules of a space. The tone increases the flow of energy and restores vibrational balance. Concentric circles of sound continue to tone a room long after the sound has faded into silence.

Historically, bells have often been associated with mysticism. Ancient metal smiths believed a kind of alchemy could be achieved during the bell-making process. In some cultures, bells were made of seven metals, as each was thought to carry the energy of a different planet, an idea originally postulated by Aristotle. When such a bell was rung, it was believed that it generated universal forces capable of aligning a dwelling space with the cosmos.

Iron was associated with Mars because of its rusty-red color and importance in ancient warfare. Lead, heavy and sluggish, was linked to Saturn. Copper is ruled by Venus and is one of the oldest metals used by men and women. It represents healing, nurturing, and youthfulness. Tin is associated with Jupiter and embodies wisdom and expansive knowledge. The metal mercury was associated with the planet Mercury because of its quick movements. Silver represented the moon, while the sun was gold. Emperors such as Holy Roman Emperor Rudolf II commissioned bells made of these seven Hermetic metals, believing that they could inspire tremendous energy.

In some traditions the ringing of metal is thought to drive away harmful spirits and negative energy. Hebrew rabbis rang bells before entering the most sacred areas of a temple to keep negativity at bay. In medieval Europe church bells rang out not only to call people to worship, but also to dispel dark forces. At the same time that sacred bells were being crafted and used in Europe, they were also being used in the temples, monasteries, and ceremonies of Japan, China, Tibet, Indonesia, India, and the Middle East. In Buddhist cultures, the sound of the bell was an offering to Buddha. Egyptian drawings on tomb walls show priests ringing bells to bestow blessings.

There are beautiful bells made all around the world. Their sounds and the metals they are made from will vary with the traditions of their origin. Any bell can be used for space clearing if you feel a sense of connection with it and love its sound. Use your intuition to find the bell that is right for you.

Balinese Bells

Balinese bells are often used for space clearing because of their superior tone. Perhaps part of the power of these remarkable bells comes from the fact that their creation is synchronized with the phases of the moon, with prayers and blessings to the gods offered at each step of the process.

Making a Balinese bell can take two months or longer, but on the auspicious day when it's finally done, a beautiful consecration ceremony calls life into the newborn bell.

Tibetan Bells

Tibetan bells (*ghanta*) are excellent tools for space clearing. These instruments were originally made in Tibet. However, after the takeover of Tibet by the Chinese, Tibetan refugees have created these highly symbolic bells in Northern India and Nepal.

Every part of a Tibetan bell is richly laden with meaning. The bell always comes with a small metal object called a *dorje*, which represents the male principle, power, and salvation.

The bell itself represents the feminine principle, wisdom, and the great void. Using the ghanta and the dorje together is thought to restore balance in a room because they represent yin and yang, the two opposing, yet harmonious, forces in the universe. Their combination creates an inner mystical unity, a balance of the two primordial creative forces of life.

Sometimes, frightening faces are imprinted on the surface of Tibetan bells. These images of gods and goddesses are intended to dispel forces of evil and darkness.

On the top of the bell is often a mandala of eight lotus leaves symbolizing the voices of the gods. Along the bottom edge of the bell are images of 51 dorjes, representing 51 challenges that can be resolved by the ringing of the bell.

Traditionally a holy man known as a *lama* would ring the bell while doing mudras (ritualistic gestures) with the dorje, which represented the dance of the gods. Tibetan bells can also be played in the same manner as a singing bowl by circling a wooden mallet around the circumference of the bell.

Decorating Your Bell with Flowers

In many traditions the bell is honored by adorning it with flowers. Tibetan and Balinese bells have openings at the top through which you can intertwine flowers. Decorating your bell with flowers is a way of honoring it, and it also adds the delicate energy of the flowers to your clearing. (See Appendix C for more information on the energy of different flowers.)

On your Blessing Altar you may want to have a stand for your bell that can also be decorated with flowers.

Tingsha Cymbals

Tingsha cymbals are two small cymbals attached by a leather thong. Tibetan in origin, they have been used by Buddhist monks as well as in shamanistic traditions. Like Tibetan bells, they are often decorated with symbolic patterns that affect the energy of the sound.

Tingshas are excellent for breaking up stagnant energy because they create a sharp piercing sound when struck at right angles to each other. They can be used for smoothing the energy after a space clearing by dangling cymbals by their cords and gently tapping them together.

CHIMING SPHERES

Harmony balls, sometimes called harmony balls, Druid balls, or Mayan balls, are small metal balls filled with tiny metal beads that roll around inside to create a magical chiming sound. These are excellent for smoothing the energy of a space after a space clearing. Cup the harmony balls in your hands and imagine they are filled with blessings for the entire household. Then take one in each hand and imagine that you are sprinkling stardust and light into the space as you shake them throughout the room. Magic!

CHIMES

Many manufacturers of wind chimes also make handheld chimes that can be used for meditation or space clearing. Because of the focused precision of their sound, these are excellent to use in a bedroom, especially after an illness or if a couple hasn't been getting along.

They are also great to use if you have been feeling unfocused and muddled in life, because they bring an energy of pure clarity and direct focus. When you use these chimes, you can sweep the walls (and the bed) in long, flowing movements.

Long sweeping movements with chimes are also effective for clearing yourself or another person after the clearing.

TUNING FORKS

Whenever you use tuning forks, you are producing pure musical resonance based on mathematical proportions known as Pythagorean tunings. These tones reflect the sonic ratios inherent in nature. The sound from tuning forks creates archetypal resonance that creates a repatterning of form and spirit.

Tuning forks are remarkable for clearing wooden antiques or solid objects. Antiques often hold residual energy, which may be negative in nature, so it is very important to clear them.

Strike the tuning fork on your hand and then take the end of the fork and place it on the antique. You will hear the sound as it vibrates and travels along the grain of the wood.

Continue to place the tuning fork on various places on the antique until you sense that the sound is clear.

When choosing a tuning fork, listen to each one first to decide which one you are the most attuned to, as this will be the best note for you to use for space clearing.

If you only choose one, choose an F sharp, as this sound opens the heart chakra.

GONGS AND SINGING BOWLS

The use of singing bowls and gongs in Asia dates back to over 3,000 years ago. Over time it was discovered that different metals created different energies in the sounds. The mixture of seven specific metals—gold, silver, nickel, copper, iron, zinc, and antimony—was believed to create a unique and powerful energy.

Many bells, gongs, and singing bowls, especially in Tibet, were created out of this combination of metals. Some of the older gongs and singing bowls (those made in Tibet before the Chinese takeover) are said to contain iron ore taken from meteorites.

Singing bowls are made of metal and can be used as a traditional gong by striking them, or you can run the wooden mallet around the rim to create a reverberating sound.

Gongs are known for the specific shapes and sounds that seem to linger in the air long after they are struck or rung. They are very powerful tools for creating sacred space.

Hanging Gongs

Hanging gongs are used in temples throughout Asia as a call to worship. It is believed that if your spirit can truly follow the sound of the gong, you will reach the Creator.

Shaped like a large platter, hanging gongs usually range from 12 to 24 inches (30 to 61 cm) in diameter. The vigor and expanse of the sounds they create can clear a room instantly.

Their ability to immediately break up and clear large amounts of negative energy make them perfect for using in very large spaces, such as a large office complex or a warehouse.

Because many of these types of gongs are large, heavy, and difficult to move about, they do not adapt easily to the clearing of smaller rooms.

A large gong can be hung from a stand and placed at the Blessing Altar. However, a small hanging gong can be used in the center of the rooms you clear by holding it by its cord, striking it, and then swinging it back and forth to send the sound in all the directions of the room.

Bowl Gongs

These types of gongs are shaped like a bowl. They range in size from 2 to 36 inches (5 to 91 cm) across. The resounding intensity that can be created when the wooden mallet strikes the rim is remarkable. It can feel as if it is vibrating deep into your core.

Bowl gongs have a penetrating sound that lingers in the air long after they are struck. Tibetan bowl gongs contain the seven metals mentioned previously and can be used as singing bowls as well as gongs.

Chinese bowl gongs do not function as singing bowls. They are the most durable of all the gongs and can usually retain their tone even after being dropped.

Bowl gongs from Japan tend to be smaller than the Tibetan or Chinese gongs and therefore are excellent for travel. They create a pure, clear tone.

Clearing a Room with a Bowl Gong

Place the bowl in your palm. (If it is a small gong, place the small cushion in your palm with the gong resting on top of it.) Whenever you enter a new room, strike the gong three times with your mallet to declare your intention. Walk around the periphery of the room, striking once wherever you feel it is needed or whenever the sound fades. Continue to move the sound throughout the space until it feels clear.

Singing Bowls

The monk cradles the large metal bowl in his hand. His fingers rest gently on the cold, smooth surface as the weight of the bowl lays heavy on his palm. Focused and deliberate, he strikes the rim with a wooden beater and slowly begins to circle its edge. A deep reverberating hum begins to build powerfully, majestically. His eyes close. His breathing becomes slow and deep. Sound fills him until he experiences disappearing into the sound. Ripples of sound undulate through him and fill the room. Softly laying down the mallet, he sits quietly until the sound becomes a whisper ... then stillness. Slowly opening his eyes, the monk looks at the space around him. The entire room seems to glisten with energy and light.

Tibetan singing bowls, sometimes called Himalayan bowls, come from Tibet, Nepal, or Northern India and have an outstanding ability to purify the energy in a home. These remarkable objects can create a sound vibration so powerful it can feel as if the walls are coming down. The vibration of the sound seems to reach deep inside your soul. Some Western doctors use singing bowls with cancer patients because they have found the sounds produced can have a beneficial impact on diseased cells. When used for spiritual purposes, the sound of the singing bowl can also project powerful energy forms.

Alexandra David-Néel, an intrepid French adventurer who spent 14 years exploring Tibet in the early 1900s, described an event in a remote lamasery. She described seeing flashes of light coming out of a singing bowl played by a lama. The holy man said the sound from the singing bowl could create shapes and even spiritual beings. He declared that one's thoughts and intention could travel on the sound of the singing bowl to create manifestations of energy.

How to Get Your Bowl to Sing

Hold your gong close to your heart. Imagine filling it with love and heart energy until you feel as though you are merging with its spirit.

When you are you ready to play, hold the bowl in one hand. Keep your fingers free from the sides of the gong, or they will interfere with its sound.

Gently tap the edge of the rim with the beater (this is said to "wake up" the bowl), and then slowly begin to circle the gong in an easy manner. Going fast does not produce a better sound.

Press firmly and evenly against the rim. If you press too lightly, the stick will vibrate against the rim and cause a rattling sound.

Allow the tone to increase in intensity. If there is an unpleasant sound of wood on metal, you can cover the part of your mallet that touches the metal with a strong, smooth tape. With large singing bowls, sometimes rubbing the stick back and forth on a small section of the rim creates a more pleasing sound than circling the entire rim.

Clearing a Room with the Singing Bowl

Slowly and carefully circle around the room, holding the bowl in one hand while you are "singing" it with the other hand.

Allow your entire body to be involved so that it is an extension of the singing bowl. Let your awareness travel on the sound to every part of the room. Visualize filling the space with vitality, light, and heartfelt energy.

If there is a place where the sound seems dull or where the energy seems stagnant, continue singing the bowl in that area until the sound is clear and bright.

Crystal Singing Bowls

Quartz crystal singing bowls have a special ability to harmonize the subtle energy of light in a room. The energy produced by them is almost alchemical in nature and can dramatically raise the consciousness of a space. Crystals have been used in spiritual practices for thousands of years. They have the ability to transmit information and energy, and hence are used in quartz radios. Crystal bowls are best used where the energy of a space is already pristine and refined, such as in a meditation room or healing center. They are less effective for clearing very dense, heavy energy.

Crystal singing bowls range in size from 6 to 20 inches (15 to 51 cm) in diameter. Different sizes produce different tones.

When selecting a crystal singing bowl, let your intuition guide you to the one that is best for you.

Because of their delicate nature, crystal singing bowls are usually played at a Blessing Altar rather than carried around the room. Alternatively, they can be carefully placed in the center of each room and played there.

These ethereal-looking singing bowls can be played by gently tapping them with a padded wooden mallet to create a pure bell-like sound. You can also circle the circumference of the crystal bowl with a rubber-coated mallet until it begins to sing.

Be careful not to allow the vibration to become too intense for too long, as this can crack the crystal. The spiraling movement of the sound creates mystic spirals in the energy of the room.

Singing Bowls and Water

One remarkable way to use a singing bowl (metal or crystal) is to fill it partway with water (ideally water that has been energized, which you'll learn how to do in Chapter 8). This combines the power of sound with the Spirit of Water.

When you circle the bowl with your mallet, the water will vibrate in small concentric patterns. Eventually small waves meet each other, and tiny sparkling droplets jump up off the surface of the water making tiny fountains.

Using a singing bowl in this way combines the energy of sound with the purifying quality of water. You can keep adding water until you reach a pitch that feels right. This is a wonderful cleansing way to harmonize the energy in a room.

The water from the bowl can be saved and used for a water-cleansing ceremony. (See Chapter 8.) If using metal, be sure to wipe it dry to prevent water stains.

Choosing a Gong or Singing Bowl

Don't be concerned about the beauty or symmetry of a gong or bowl when you first look at it. Regardless of its outward appearance, the gong that is meant to be yours will seem to emanate a unique inner beauty.

Take the gong and hold it close to your heart chakra and gently strike it. If it is truly yours, it will seem to resonate through your entire body.

When choosing a metal gong, some people prefer a hand-hammered one to a machine-made, symmetrical one.

Although hand-hammered gongs are usually older, the sound and spirit of a new gong can equal an old one. It is a matter of personal preference. Most metal gongs are sold by weight, so heavier ones will be more costly.

The purchase of a singing bowl will usually come with a beater. This wooden mallet should be heavy and smooth, as the denser the wood and the smoother the surface, the better the tone produced in the bowl.

You may also want to purchase an additional beater covered with felt or leather for striking your gong rather than circling it. Different mallets will bring out different sounds from your gong or singing bowl, so you may want to have several of them.

MUSICAL INSTRUMENTS

As mentioned, any instrument can be used for space clearing. A piano or harp played with a focused intention to clear a space can do a magnificent job. One limitation with large instruments is that they cannot be taken from room to room.

However, with a strong intention, a piano can clear an entire small wooden house as the sound penetrates through the wood. A flute, whether made of silver, wood, or reed, is very well suited for space clearing.

As with any tool, the most important elements are your focused attention and the attunement of your body to the spirit of the tool.

Anything that makes a pleasant, soothing, or even amusing sound can be effectively used in space clearing.

Little "squeakies," the kind of toys made for babies or animals, although not technically a musical instrument, are nonetheless excellent for dispelling heavy or overly serious energy. They bring a spirit of laughter to a space and are very good for children's rooms or anywhere you want to instill an atmosphere of fun and light-hearted joy. In fact, laughter can also be an extraordinary space clearing tool.

CLAPPING

If you don't have any space clearing tools with you and you need a quick fix right now, no problem. Use your hands!

Walk around the circumference of the room with one hand extended to sense the energy. Anyplace where the energy feels stuck, give three swift claps. Sense the energy and then clap again to see if the energy has changed. The sound should be crisper and brighter the second time. Once the area is clear, take your hand and smooth the energy and continue on. (See page 14 for a reminder of how to smooth the energy of a space.)

CHANTING, SINGING, AND TONING

One of the most sacred and ancient uses of the human voice is for clearing and blessing a space. Chanting, singing, and toning are time-honored methods for clearing energy. The sound resonates directly through your body so that it becomes the space clearing tool.

Chanting

Chanting is a powerful tool because it combines sound vibration with sacred words. In ancient times, sages and mystics understood the great power of words.

Chants were created to combine a powerful meaning of a word with a particular vibration of a sound. You can re-create this tradition by repetitively chanting words that have a special meaning for you.

For example, you could chant the word *peace* over and over again in your space clearing with the intention that each of the occupants of your household would feel at home with themselves wherever they are.

Om

One of the best-known examples of chanting is the use of the mantra *Om*. This powerful Sanskrit word signifies the sound of the Divine and the totality of all life. It is believed that this sound has the ability to release suffering and create profound transformation.

To create this sound, simply relax, breathe, and gently exhale the sound "Ah-Ohhh-Mmmm." Let yourself merge with the sound until you sense that you are filling the space around you. Go slowly. Allow the sound to find its own octave and rhythm.

Pronounced "Ah-Ohhh-Mmm Mah-Nee Pad-May Hum," this Sanskrit mantra is translated as "the jewel in the lotus." It is believed that this combination of sound links you directly to the Creator, empowers anything that you do, and activates compassion and love both within you and in the space around you.

Om: The totality of all of life

Mani: The jewel symbolizing that which is of most precious value

Padme: The lotus rising out of darkness into the light as it moves up through the muddy pond; a symbol of awakening wisdom

Hum: The sound of this word awakens consciousness

Toning

Toning is the creation of tones or vowel-like sounds without the structure of a chant. It is a primal sound resonating through your entire body.

Toning can be extraordinarily powerful. To tone, reach deep inside of yourself to find your primal sound. It is that most essential sound within you, the quintessential expression of who you are.

One way to find your sound is to go up and down the musical scale, humming until you find a note that seems to resonate through your entire body. Once you have found this, stand in the middle of the room, open your mouth, and allow this single note to flow out from your body to fill the entire space. As you tone, you may find that the pitch of your sound spontaneously changes.

Sometimes a room will respond to a lower note first, and then later you may find yourself using higher notes as the vibratory energy of the room raises. You will know when the space has been toned because it will feel balanced and calm.

You can also tone an individual object in a room. Do this by bringing your mouth close to it and then cup your hands by your mouth to direct the sound toward the object.

Because this mantra has the power to awaken spiritual forces within any space, it is an excellent way to end and begin any space clearing.

Tibetan Prayer Wheel while Chanting

Mystical swirling Tibetan Prayer Wheels send prayers of peace out to the four corners of the universe. These wonderful tools, which were once used only in Tibetan monasteries, are now being used by space clearers. Atop an ornately decorated wooden handle rests a metal cylinder, which contains thousands of hand printed prayers. (You can also take one apart to add your own prayers.) Every squeaky swirl of the wheel sends these prayers into the home.

Spinning the prayer wheel as you chant is a very effective way of deepening the power of the chant. These are also excellent to use for blessing the land around a home.

Hey-Ya

Although there are over 500 recognized Native American tribes in the United States, each with their own traditions and language, there is a mantra-like chant that is used in most of these tribes: *Hey-Ya.*

This word calls Spirit and is similar in sound and meaning to words used in other earth-based cultures around the world. A repetitive chant of this word before, during, and after your space clearing can dispel stuck energy and call the natural forces of the earth into balance in a dwelling. The emphasis is on the "Hey" with a forcible amount of air being projected as you say it.

Recorded Music

Sometimes music can be a helpful adjunct to space clearing. A very soothing melody, ambient music, or recorded sacred chanting can form a powerful backdrop to the clearing that you are doing. It can help you remain focused while you work and help balance the energy in an unoccupied room.

However, there are times when music can distract your ability to sense energy fields, so it's important to be aware of whether the music is enhancing or detracting from your space clearing. You should be guided by your intuition to decide what is best. If you do use a music player during your clearing, enclose it in something beautiful so that it matches the sacred energy of your Blessing Altar.

RATTLES AND DRUMS

Drumming speaks to us directly of the basic rhythm of life. It re-creates the primordial pulse of life, as we first knew it in the womb. The beating of the drum can align a living space to the universal tempo within all things.

In ancient times, drumming was used to sanctify and cleanse homes before moving in and after sickness or death. Tibetan, Japanese, African, Chinese, Indonesian, Middle Eastern, Innuit, Saami, and Native American cultures have all used the drum to bring harmony to living spaces.

Rattles

Rattles are an excellent complement to the use of a drum in space clearing. While a drum is excellent for breaking up accumulated energy, the rattle is good for smoothing energy afterward. It operates on the same principles as the drum but is more smoothing in nature.

You can even make your own rattles in a very simple and budget-friendly way by using the hollow plastic eggs that are usually sold around Easter. Fill them with tiny decorative beads used in crafts called seed beads. Close them securely with tape or glue, and then decorate or paint them.

These simple tools can smooth the creases out of any space.

Types of Drums

The most common type of drum for space clearing is the frame drum, which is a handheld drum about 12 to 15 inches (30 to 38 cm) in diameter. However, other kinds of drums can be used, such as the African drum, which is usually carried with a strap over the shoulders.

Irish drums (*bodhráns*) can be used both for toning as well as for rhythmic cadence. They have a magnificent ability to amplify the sound of your toning or chanting in a space.

To use the bodhrán in this way, hold it close to your mouth without actually touching it with your lips. Cup your hand against your mouth, directing the sound to the drum skin and begin to tone. The skin of the drum will vibrate with your sound, radiating the sound into the room.

In Australian Aborigine tradition, click sticks are used instead of the drum. The rhythmic sound of click sticks produces the same shifts of energy as the sound of a drum.

It is easy to make your own click sticks (also sometimes called clap sticks) from wooden dowels or two sticks you find in nature. You can use them plain or you can sand them until they are smooth and then decorate them. They can be painted or carved with symbols that are sacred to you. The most important thing is the sound. It should be sharp and crisp.

How to Use Drums for Space Clearing

Different rhythms will produce different effects on you and the space you are clearing. Instead of deciding what tempo you want to use, let your drum tell you what to do! It will tell you the cadence, strength of beat, and even where on the drum surface to strike as you allow its energy to flow through you.

As you begin, hold your drum close to your heart and imagine that you are breathing life into it.

Hold an intention of your desire for your clearing. Then rub your hand around the surface of the drum to warm and greet it.

If no rhythm emerges immediately, begin with a two-beat. This is the same rhythm as a heartbeat and will allow you to enter into a deeper state of consciousness where you can sense subtle energy.

As you begin to walk around the perimeter of the room, notice any differences in the sound of the drum. If there are places where the sound is dull, pay attention to those areas. Often varied rhythms will spontaneously occur as you enter different areas of a room. You will intuitively find the exact rhythms that are needed for each part of the room.

An ancient Cherokee saying says, "The Sun and the Moon are the drumsticks playing upon the Earth, bringing harmony and peace to all the Earth's children." Drums carry the heartbeat of Mother Earth or the Spirit of Life. The drum is feminine, and the drumstick is masculine. Bringing them together helps harmonize the yin and yang forces of the universe. Drums are circles of power, and they are highly respected in native and ancient cultures.

The difference between drums and other space clearing tools is that drums can break up heavy, dense, thick energy quickly. Bells, chimes, essential oils, feathers, and incense are well suited for more subtle energy.

Care for Your Drum

It's important to care for your drum. The more attention you give it, the better it will be at shifting energy. The tension of the head of the drum will fluctuate in response to weather conditions: the humidity and heat in the air. If you live in a damp climate and your drum sounds a bit flat, this is natural. You may need to gently warm your drum in front of a fire or over a lamp, taking care not to burn the hide. If your drum sounds like a tin can, it may be too dry. In this case, you can gently mist it with water until the tone you desire is obtained.

A drum should be kept in a place of honor (either hung securely on a wall, stored in a beautiful bag or case, or placed on display with its face up). Drums should be stored in a dry area out of direct sunlight.

Make sure that you spend time honoring the animal and the tree spirits from which the drum was made. This is essential to gain the best energy. (It is important to note, however, that there are wonderful synthetic drums now available with excellent sound.)

How to Drum

Hold your drum close to your heart and imagine love flowing to your drum. Greet your drum by slowly rubbing your hand around in a circle on your drum. Address your drum by name or with a reverent title.

Be still and allow the energy inside of you to build.

When the energy is at its peak, express it as a shout or just begin to drum. This calls Spirit and asks for assistance. Now begin drumming.

Keep your drumstick hand really loose. Allow your wrist to be flexible so the movement comes from the wrist instead of the arm.

Remember that the heartbeat is a good rhythm to begin with. It's a primal sound for humans, as we hear it in the womb. This aligns and balances the yin and yang forces of the universe.

Allow your breath to deepen and your body to relax.

Eventually allow the energy and feeling inside of you to come through your drumming. Trust your intuition. Get out of the way, and allow the drumming to happen. Connect with the spirit of the drum.

End as you began. As the energy builds to a peak, let out a shout as a thank-you to Great Spirit for assisting you, or simply be still and allow Spirit to fill the space and you.

CHAPTER 7

Alchemy
of
Air *and* Fire

Fire . . . smoke . . . feathers . . . this triad of elements has been used in clearing rites since the dawn of time. Used today, they link our lives to those of our ancient ancestors.

A candle's flame, the gentle plume of smoke rising from a stick of incense or burning herbs, the delicate strength of a feather—all of these are universal symbols of our connection to Spirit, archetypes recognized by people around the world.

Different cultures of different time periods may disagree about which herbs, feathers, and rituals are best; nevertheless, there is an abundance of commonalties between these surface details that transcend their differences.

Fire, smoke, and feathers have been used separately and together for thousands of years to purify and transform energy, to enter an altered state of consciousness, and for the healing of bodies and minds. Fire burns away impurities, both physical and spiritual. The trail of incense smoke carries our prayers to heaven. The feather fascinates us because of its intimate connection to an element so different from our own. As the bird soars toward the heavens, so the soul longs to fly home, to the ultimate source of everything, a place where inner and outer, above and below, join into one.

When you use the tools of fire, smoke, and feathers in your space clearing work, you will be creating a haven of balance, harmony, and healing.

TRANSFORMATIVE MAGIC OF FIRE

Since earliest times, man has been fascinated by fire. An essential ally in the daily struggle for survival, fire has sustained us—body and soul—from the beginning. Small wonder then that art, religion, dance, myth, and poetry have celebrated the amazing phenomenon of fire throughout the ages.

Ceremonies using fire are some of the most powerful for instantly clearing the energy of an environment. Fire consumes, transforms, and destroys, even as it clears the way for the new. Fire is primal. It is pure energy, passion, transcendence, and inspiration.

Fire is a living being. It is no less alive than the very earth that we walk on, the air we breathe, and the water we drink. Fire Spirits are filled with warmth, passion, and zest. The very act of lighting a candle or a stick of incense can cause a change in your state of awareness. It can uplift the energy in a room and can connect you to the living spirit of fire.

The use of fire in the home for spiritual cleansing and dedication is one of the oldest, surest, and most immediate of space clearing techniques, for fire can be a catalyst between the known and the unknown. It transcends yet embraces form. It is the absolute purifier and transformer as it consumes its fuel.

One of our greatest symbols for transformation is the phoenix rising anew from the ashes left by raging flames. The phoenix does not merely rise as a newer edition of its previous form but also flies forth exalted and glorified, a hallowed spirit. Alchemists held that fire was "the agent of transmutation," believing that all things come from, and return to, fire.

You can also use fire for dedicating and invoking fresh, clear energy into a room once the room has been cleared. The most common means of using fire for bringing forth energy into a room is through the use of candles.

CANDLES

When you begin your space clearing, place a candle on the Blessing Altar and keep it burning throughout your ceremony. The light and energy from this candle will be at the heart of all you do and will help you manifest your intention. Before you begin, take a moment to let your hands absorb the warmth of the candle's halo. Cup your fingers around the light and draw its spirit to your body. Focus on your intention for the clearing. Brush the energy of the fire over your head and body with light, quick movements to cleanse your aura.

You can also purify the energy of your tools by holding them above the candle's flame. (Be sure not to hold them so close that they catch fire or become overheated.) As you pass each tool through the purifying energy of the fire's warmth, let your intention center on your purpose for the clearing and the part that the tool will play in it.

You can also light a small votive candle and leave it in each room you clear. Allowing it to burn to extinction will deepen and set the energy that you have created there.

An alternative option is to place a small votive in the center of a flower offering in each room. To create a flower offering, as mentioned in Chapter 2, take a saucer and place the votive candle in the center, surrounded by fresh flowers. You can put a small amount of water in the saucer to keep the flowers fresh. Doing this combines the power of the fire's purifying energy with the healing power of water and the gentle and beautiful energy of the flowers.

To turn an ordinary votive candle into an aromatherapy candle, light it and wait until the wax has become partially liquefied. Then blow it out and add a few drops of an essential oil to the liquid wax. Allow it to cool before putting it away to use at your clearing. This is an inexpensive alternative to more costly aromatherapy products. (For a guide to choosing flowers and essential oils, see Appendices C and D.)

Types of Candles

There are numerous types of candles that you can use for invoking new energy. Most candles are made from beeswax, paraffin, or soy; some drip and some are drip-free. Though a candle from any material can be used, I prefer, whenever possible, to use candles that have been handmade and hand-dipped, since a human being has participated in their creation.

Whenever possible, I like to use beeswax instead of petroleum-based paraffin candles. Although they are more expensive and can sometimes be difficult to obtain, they have a remarkably pure energy and high-frequency vibration. The delicate aroma they emit when burning brings to a room all of the golden clarity of amber honey, the fresh energy generated by open fields full of herbs and flowers. This spirit of creation is released once again as the candle is burned.

All the different styles of candles—tapers, straight candles, glass-encased candles, and votives—can be used according to your needs.

How to Use Fire: Focusing Intention and Intensity of Purpose

Whenever you use fire for space clearing and for hallowed purposes, focus your intention, especially right before you light it. This means that prior to lighting the candle, you should very clear on your reasons for lighting it. Focus your attention on your desired results. The second step, intensity of purpose, requires that you intensely concentrate or project your purpose while lighting the candle. For a familiar example of this concept, you can look at the Western cultural tradition of making a wish (focusing attention/ intention) while concentrating (intensity of purpose) on blowing out candles on a birthday cake.

Once a room is cleared, you are ready to dedicate the energy of the room with your candle. Hold the candle in your hands. Take just a moment to center yourself and imagine yourself surrounded by radiant peace. Then focus your intention on the results that you desire for the room. You might desire that the room be filled with light and warmth. Or you might focus your intention on protection and safety.

Then bless your candle by holding it next to the center of your chest, your heart chakra. Or you might hold it above your head asking for the blessings of Spirit, or whatever higher power you believe in. There is no right way to bless your candle. As always, follow the path that feels best to you and follow the wisdom of your heart.

As you are holding the candle, take three deep, full breaths and begin to feel a quietness expand inside of you. Allow a "feeling" of the results that you intend for the room to fill you, and then begin to visualize the room filled with that feeling. When this feeling/visualization has reached a clear intensity, then light the wick of the candle, feeling the intensity of your purpose. In that moment the candle's flame acts as a magnifier and projects your thoughts and feelings onto the room.

Now simply gaze into the flame and allow your intention to fill the room. You could even say aloud or silently several times a word that expresses your wishes for the room. For example, say, "Peace. Peace. Peace." With the candle being a focus point, know that energy generated by your intention and intensity is filling the room.

Now just let go and relax. This is when the true magic occurs.

Thank Spirit and leave the candle burning (in a safe place, of course). The energy you have generated will continue as long as the flame burns. The continuous flame in your home is like a spiritual presence projecting the intention of your specific dedication for as long as it burns. If it is not a candle intended for continuous burning, extinguish it when you go to sleep or whenever you leave the house.

In some traditions, a candle used for room clearing is never blown out. You either squeeze it out or use a candle snuffer. This is done out of respect for the Fire Spirits.

CANDLES AND THE POWER OF COLORS

Combining the power of fire with the energy of color can be particularly potent, as there is no doubt that color affects us all. When you choose candles for clearing the energy in your home, I suggest you pay attention to the colors that you are choosing.

Color is very personal, so it is important that you pick whichever colored candles feel good to you, rather than always following a prescribed formula. If you find it helpful, refer to the color guide in Appendix A as well as the information that follows. Remember that there may also be colors that I haven't mentioned that feel right to you for a particular room.

For example, I sometimes use pink candles in my living room because I associate the color pink with love, and it gives a warm feeling in this much used room. In my meditation room, I often burn turquoise candles because I associate turquoise with my Native American roots. In addition, I personally find the color combination of blue and green very soothing.

Red Candles

Use a red candle in a room if you want to stimulate physical activity.

For example, if you have a room or a place in your home where you have exercise equipment and you want to increase your physical strength, you may want to burn a red candle in that area. Or, alternatively, if sensuality has waned in your relationship, you may want to burn a red candle in your bedroom and dedicate it to passion.

Prayer that can be said while lighting a red candle:

I dedicate this candle to courage, strength, and passion.
May the blazing life force of a red setting sun fill this room now!
May all who enter this place be filled with strength,
determination, and zeal.

Orange Candles

Use an orange candle in a room where family and friends will be gathering. For example, you might want to burn an orange candle just before a party to stimulate camaraderie and enthusiasm in the room. You could dedicate this candle to joy and happiness for the evening ahead.

Prayer that can be said while lighting an orange candle:

*I dedicate this candle to boundless joy and optimism.
May the beauty of an orange poppy opening to the morning sun
fill all who enter here with warmth of companionship
and freedom of self-expression.*

Yellow Candles

Use a yellow candle in a room where you or your children study, or to stimulate philosophical conversation or increased concentration.

Prayer that can be said while lighting a yellow candle:

*I dedicate this yellow candle to the clarity of sunlight. May this
room be filled with joy and clear focus. Bring wisdom, joyous
communication, and good luck to all who enter here.*

Green Candles

Green candles are beneficial in any area where the family spends time. They are also helpful when used in the room of someone who is ill. Green candles stimulate feelings of balance, harmony, peace, hope, growth, and healing.

Prayer that can be said while lighting a green candle:

*I dedicate this green candle to healing, rebirth, and abundance.
May the color of spring leaves unfurling fill this room with
healing, balance, renewal, and vigor.*

Blue Candles

Blue candles are excellent for bedrooms or for rooms where meditation is done because of the relaxing energy of this color.

Prayer that can be said while lighting a blue candle:

I dedicate this candle to serenity and inner truth. May all who enter this room be touched by the gentle blue of the wide-open sky, and may this room be filled with Spirit and peace.

Purple Candles

As with the blue candles, the effects of purple are soothing. In addition, this color is often associated with psychic awareness and intuition.

I recommend lavender and violet candles for meditation rooms or for your home altar.

Prayer that can be said while lighting a purple candle:

I dedicate this candle to inner visions and inner truth. May the deep purple of the evening sky bring a deepening of intuition and peace to all who enter this room.

White Candles

White is the color that encompasses all colors. White candles can be used in any room at any time.

Prayer that can be said while lighting a white candle:

I dedicate this candle to spiritual awakening and attunement. May the purity of the white snow in wintertime fill all who enter here with divine realization.

Seven-Day Candles

Burning a seven-day candle is an easy way to maintain the balance of energy in your home after you have performed space clearing rituals of any kind. These candles, which also come in 10-day and 14-day varieties, are designed to be left burning continuously for the specified number of days in the name. They are quite large and thick and come in tall, heatproof glass containers. Look for them in candle shops as well as religious and spiritual supply stores.

These religious candles usually come in various colored glass containers. However, if you are unable to find this sort of candle in the colors you desire, try putting a plain one inside a tube of colored cellophane. Be sure you allow adequate air space around the container, so that the cellophane does not become hot.

You can decorate these types of candles, write affirmations on the side of the glass, decorate them with beads, or even melt some of the wax and then add essential oils as the wax is cooling... voilà, instant aromatherapy candles.

It is important to keep your candles in a safe place, away from fabrics and flammable materials, to minimize any danger of fire. I like to keep at least one seven-day candle burning continuously in my home, for it greatly increases the living spirit in my surroundings. It gives off a warm and welcoming feeling to anyone walking into a home or room where such a candle has been maintaining a silent vigil.

SPIRIT SMOKE

A delicate plume of smoke curling upward through still air evokes immediate and powerful associations with ritual, purification, and spiritual connections. For thousands of years, humans everywhere have burned herbs, scented wood, resins, and other aromatic substances as a way to channel their hopes, prayers, and dreams to the realm of Spirit.

Smoke purifies and transports. It transforms the ordinary into the sacred. It speaks directly to one of our most powerful and primordial senses: the sense of smell, a sense integrally connected to buried memories, emotions, and perception.

Because of this connection, the use of smoke can powerfully and instantly change the energy in a room. It's also believed that our prayers can travel on the plume of the smoke and the blessings from the Creator can descend down the plume as well.

SMUDGING

In smudging, the smoke produced by burning herbs is used to purify and transform the energy of a space, to alter consciousness, or to clear the personal energy of yourself or another. Although the practice of smudging is pan-global, in the Western world two of the most common herbs used for this purpose are common sage and cedar, both of which are very potent purifiers. You can also use rosemary, spruce, pine, fir, lavender, mullein, mugwort, juniper, palo santo, myrrh, frankincense, peppermint, catnip, incense, and many more. Research the history and environmental impact of any herbs you choose, so as to make more sustainable and culturally sensitive choices.

Smudge Sticks, Loose Herbs, and Pieces of Resin

Herbs can be bunched together and then wrapped tightly with string to create a bundle, which is one of the easiest and most common ways to use herbs for smudging. The dried smudge bundle is first lit and then extinguished, leaving the still-smoldering herbs to give off their pungent smoke.

Herbs in leaf form, frankincense, myrrh, and other resinous materials can also be used for smudging. To do this they must be burned in a fireproof bowl that is large enough to contain at least several inches of soil, sand, or salt. The fireproof bowl must also be placed on some fireproof surface in the unlikely event that the heat causes it to crack.

A small charcoal tablet or briquette is first lit with a candle or lighter and is then placed in the bowl. It is essential to use metal tongs when lighting the charcoal because it will be become extremely hot very quickly. In addition, the part of the tongs in contact with your hands must be covered with fabric or leather, because they too will become hot from the charcoal. The charcoal sometimes emits large sparks when you are lighting it, so be sure you light it in a safe place away from anything that could catch fire from a stray spark.

Once the charcoal tablet is burning in the fireproof bowl, you can place herbs or resinous incense on it with the tongs. Usually this creates a volume of smoke. Carefully carry the bowl into each room so that the smoke fills every corner of the home. Hold the thought that the smoke purifies and blesses everything that it touches. It's important to be conscientious of smoke detectors.

Once you are done with your ceremony, lift the charcoal briquette out of the bowl with your metal tongs and extinguish it in a container of water. A charcoal briquette and smoldering herbs can both appear to be out, but they have been known to spontaneously reignite hours later, so caution about this is essential.

Caution: When you are burning herbs, be very careful if you fan them with a feather or fan. The movement can cause smoldering leaves to fly away from you, trailing embers into the room and thus creating a potential fire hazard.

How to Obtain Herbs for Smudging

Bundles of herbs for smudging are easy to obtain through many mail-order businesses, but the most powerful herbs to use are those that you have grown, gathered, and bundled yourself. Doing this provides a more intimate connection with the plant than is possible to get in any other way. Prayers are given at each stage of the process for the health of the plant and to thank it for its giveaway.

The best time to gather your own herbs for smudging is at dawn, when the sun is just peeking over the horizon.

In that moment, slowly and deliberately walk toward the plant you have chosen. Kneel and give thanks for its gift to you. Then gently place your hands on the branch you have chosen to use for your ceremony. Ask permission from the plant to use a part of it, and then wait in silence until you sense that this permission is given. If you do not sense this, then move on to another plant and ask again.

Never take more than a small portion of a plant. It is essential to leave most of it so that it can go on growing in health. Also, offer a gift in return for what you are taking. In some traditions, a bit of hair or some cornmeal is offered to the plant and the soil as a prayer of thanksgiving is said. Herbs gathered in this way have a remarkable and unique power.

INCENSE

Incense is a powerful, ancient tool for space clearing. It has been universally used for large and small rituals, from the high mass of the Catholic Church to the private use of incense on a personal altar. The smell of incense in a room can magically change the mood there. It can create a sense of magic, a connection to inner wisdom. In past times it was used before moving into a new home, and to disinfect a room after sickness or a death. Priests and priestesses used it before sacred ceremonies as a way to clear the space and invoke the gods.

The energy of incense varies with the place of its origin, the manner in which it is made, and its ingredients. It is important to use the purest quality incense you can obtain, and to use incense made from natural rather than synthetic materials.

Incense is commonly made from various parts of plants, wood, tree resins, seeds, leaves, and evergreen needles. Each culture has its own special varieties for which it is known. Frankincense, myrrh, sandalwood, patchouli, cinnamon, cedar, and sage are some of the best known. Sticks, cones, leaves, resins, needles, pellets, tablets—the forms which incense comes in are multitudinous. It can be fun to experiment with different kinds to see which you prefer and which ones work the best for the clearing work that you do. Here is a brief glimpse into the diverse world of incense. The ones listed herein are only a tiny fraction of the varieties available from many cultures.

Indian Incense

India is known as the Mother of Fragrances, so called because of the incredible wealth of scents that are such a vital part of its culture. Probably the single most important incense out of all these myriad fragrances is sandalwood. Considered vital for the optimal passage of a soul from one life to the next, it is considered a remedy for many ailments in Ayurvedic medicine. Sandalwood is excellent for bringing relaxation and peace into a home. Other common Indian scents include elemi, common myrrh, benzoin, patchouli, and dammar.

Japanese Incense

The Japanese have developed their practice of "listening to incense" over thousands of years. Elevated to the status of a great art form, an elaborate ceremony for savoring the pleasures of scent is called *koh-do*, which translates as "the journey of the fragrance."

Although most of the ingredients of Japanese incense are not native to that country and must be imported, the subtle blends and meticulous attention paid to their combination have made Japanese incense some of the finest in the world.

The most important source of scents in Koh culture is aloeswood, sometimes referred to as agarwood. Ancient records describe a piece of aloeswood washing up on the shore of Awaji island in the 6th century. The villagers did not recognize it as anything special and burned it along with other driftwood. But its fragrance was so startlingly lovely that it was taken and presented as a gift to the empress. Since that time, aloeswood has been considered highly valuable for its enchanting aroma. Other common ingredients of Japanese incense include cinnamon, sandalwood, cloves, Japanese anise, and camphor.

Native American "Incense"

Underlying the Native American use of fragrant woods and needles is the belief in the living spirit within all things. As the plant-based scent is burned, it is believed that the inherent wisdom within the plant is imparted to the person burning it. If the individual doing the space clearing has an open heart, secrets will be shared about what is good for her people, and what is needed for healing the dwelling. Thanks should be humbly offered to the spirit of the sage or cedar for gifts received. This is the Native American way of respect and harmony.

The smoke of the dried plant is also thought to carry prayers to the Creator and is a channel for blessings to flow back to the earth. Thus, the circle is completed. In a traditional Native American space clearing ceremony, sacred herbs are burned in a shell or earthenware, which is first offered to the sacred Four Directions (east, south, west, and north), before being used in the rite. In this way the connection between people, the earth, and the spirits is honored. Tobacco, sage, sweetgrass, pinion (pine), cedar, and juniper are some of the herbs most commonly used for Native American burning-plants ceremonies.

Middle Eastern Incense Resins

Steeped in mystery and historical significance, one of the most powerful cleansing resins is frankincense. The tree it comes from grows in the rocky desert of the Middle East in a narrow strip of land only 9 miles (14.5 km) long that contains the exact minerals that give frankincense its delicate fragrance. This remarkable resin has unprecedented healing properties. It acts as a disinfectant that has been shown to kill bacteria and heal wounds. It is believed that it was used in temples, churches, and mosques because it reduced the danger of infection and disease when many people gathered together for services.

Some people develop an aversion to frankincense as it reminds them of negative childhood experiences in church. This is unfortunate because it is one of the strongest substances on our planet for cleansing a space. In addition, it can open subtle energy channels for spiritual and even cosmic energy to pour into an environment. Used in combination with myrrh (which was considered to have "feminine" energy while frankincense was considered "masculine"), it can be a powerful tool to clear and bless a dwelling.

FEATHERS

A beautiful companion of fire and smoke, and a symbol of power, grace, and freedom, the amazing feather has been a favorite tool of shamans since the beginning of human history.

Because the quill of the feather is an open tube, many cultures have believed that it serves as a channel for prayers and energy. When worn on one's head, energy moves through the body of a person, through the quill, and is ultimately channeled directly to the Creator. A multitude of blessings flows in return from this ultimate source back down through the center of the feather and into the heart of the one holding it.

Because of its delicate attunement to the finer aspects of energy, feathers are useful for all phases of the clearing, from the initial assessment to the clearing and balancing of energy. Many people have found that it is easier to assess the energy of a room, object, or person using a feather than with their hands alone. This is because the subtle nature of the feather's energy makes it able to tune in to the finest shifts of energy in the environment.

The feather can allow you to tune in to levels of awareness that may have previously been inaccessible to you. And a single feather can clear an entire home if your intention is clearly focused.

Clearing Your Aura with a Feather

When using a feather to clear your energy, you will want to begin by first taking the time to deeply connect with the energy of the feather. Hold it next to your heart, and imagine yourself merging with the energy of the feather and the spirit of the bird from which it came. As you become one, together you will work to achieve the magic of the clearing.

Once you are completely clear about your intention, you will know that you're ready to begin. Start by using short flicking movements, going from head to toe over your entire body.

Whenever you sense that there is stagnant energy someplace (this will feel "sticky" or somehow just "wrong" as you move the feather along), concentrate your efforts there with short, quick movements to break up the stagnant energy. Once you feel the energy beginning to move, switch to long, smooth strokes of the feather to smooth the energy out and increase its balanced flow. You should feel very different when you are complete.

Clearing a Room with Feathers

The same principles apply to clearing a room with a feather. Begin with short flicking movements as you circle the room in a clockwise direction.

Wherever you sense a pooling of stagnant energy, chop into it with the feather to break it up and get it moving. Then make your motions with the feather longer, slower, and more fluid to encourage the influx of the healthy flow of balanced, calm energy into the room.

Using Feathers with Smoke

A traditional and highly effective way to clear a room is to combine the movements of the feather with smoke. This is one of the most powerful ways to balance the energy of any room.

The natural channeling powers of the feather combined with the healing spiritual properties of the burning incense or herbs can create a sense of sacred space in a very deep and immediate way.

To clear a room or a person with a feather and smoke, hold a bowl containing sand and the smoking herbs/incense in your non-dominant hand. Make sure that the bowl is deep enough to prevent any sparks flying out of it into the room. You will also want to be sure that the bowl contains enough sand so that it does not become so hot that it burns your hand. Use the feather in your dominant hand to move the smoke over the body of a person or throughout a room.

Use the same movements as described above—short flicking motions followed by long sweeping ones. The beauty of the plumes of smoke being moved about in this way is very healing.

Trust your intuition about the best method for moving the feather, and in the deepest sense let the feather decide what is needed.

Cleansing Your Aura with Smoke

Place a bowl of smoking herbs or incense on a table, then draw the smoke to your body with a feather or your cupped hands to cleanse and purify your aura before beginning your clearing. Clear your mind and focus on your intention as you draw the smoke down your body.

Kinds of Feathers

Every feather has its own unique energy, and knowing the qualities of each as well as the bird that it comes from will let you use them to their best advantage in your clearing.

Please note: Governments often have very specific legal restrictions regulating the possession of bird feathers. These laws are intended to protect species that might otherwise go extinct. Out of respect for these animals and our environment, it is essential that you first research what regulations relate to possession and use of feathers in your area.

The following is a list of some feathers and their attributes. It is not complete. When you are trying to decide if a particular feather is right for you, tune in to its energy. Let your intuition tell you what is best.

- *Turkey:* An excellent feather for space clearing. In Native American traditions, it is considered to be the "giveaway bird," because it gives its life for the benefit of others. This energy will greatly enhance your work as you provide the service of space clearing for the benefit of those around you.

- *Raven and crow:* Linked to the inner life and secret realms. A powerful and ancient energy.

- *Eagle and hawk:* Soaring and powerful. Calls the energy of the sun.

- *Owl:* Invokes the energy of the moon and is associated with wisdom and ancient mysteries.

- *Goose:* Geese mate for life and live in highly socialized flocks; therefore, their feathers are linked to loyalty and family ties.

Caring for Feathers

Keep the feathers you use for space clearing in a cherished place. Treating your feathers with the respect they deserve enhances their effectiveness. You will want to "feed" your feathers by occasionally dusting them with a bit of cornmeal and then flicking it off. Doing this symbolically feeds the spirit of the bird and replenishes the feather's energy.

Many birds have insect parasites that may be present in feathers. If left untreated, these mites will eventually eat your feathers away and destroy their beauty and usefulness. Storing your feathers in an airtight box in the freezer for six months will prevent this, as will storing them in cedar, sage, borax, and especially tobacco.

Types of Feathers for Space Clearing

There are three traditional forms of feathers for space clearing: single feathers, feather fans, and wings. A single unadorned feather is an excellent tool for space clearing. You can also decorate a feather by wrapping the exposed end of the quill with leather or cloth. This in turn can be decorated with beads and strips of leather.

A feather fan is usually made from several feathers gathered together and secured with a piece of leather or a wooden base. The feather fan has a wider surface for moving energy throughout a room. Fans can also be made very beautiful with a variety of decorative methods, from painting and beading to exquisite embroidery and leatherwork.

When you are using an entire wing from a bird, it will usually be from a goose or turkey, as these are more easily obtained. Occasionally you may come across a raven or owl wing, although of course whenever you are working with wings from wild birds, the previously noted restrictions must be respected. It is also very important to make sure that the wing has been properly cured and treated for insect infestation before use.

Wings move air and energy in a very powerful way, and they are also very beautiful. They call to mind angelic energy and are associated with these beings.

FANS

Various cultures and traditions use fans made of bamboo, wood, paper, or woven grasses for space clearing. If you are unable to obtain feathers or choose not to use feathers, fans can be employed in the same manner as feathers.

In ancient China, women used fans to avert negative energies. With a subtle twist of the wrist, negative energy was flicked away. To use a fan in this way for space clearing, use swift, concise movements with the fan held either sideways or downward.

"BREATH OF SPIRIT"

One very powerful space clearing ceremony that utilizes the alchemy of air is the shamanistic way of "breathing a room," which is sometimes called the Breath of Spirit.

To use this potent technique, take a few very deep, full breaths through your nose to center yourself. Know that your breath can connect you to the divine forces in the universe. Imagine that you are breathing in *prana*, or life-force energy, with every breath. Then, as you slowly move about a room, if you find an area that seems murky or full of stagnant energy, you can use a series of short, quick breaths blown out through your mouth directly at the area that feels stuck.

Once you have broken up the stagnant energy in this way, you can use long out-flowing breaths to smooth and refine the energy. Your hands follow the movement of air created by your breathing to enhance the effectiveness of this technique.

CONNECTING WITH THE SPIRIT OF FIRE

Fire enthralls us with its primal essence. In ancient times it was thought to be a gift of the gods that carried the spark of life and the power of renewal. We honor the influence of fire because it can maintain life . . . and it can also destroy it. It is the warmth of the hearth, but also the lightening bolt striking from the sky. Fire can purify and transform but it can also annihilate. It is the etheric light of the aurora borealis and the erupting volcano. It is the mediator between the visible and the invisible; between energy and form.

The ultimate symbol of fire is the sun. To many ancient people the sun was not only the sacred source of light and warmth, it was honored as a god. The Egyptians called the sun god Ra. In Greek mythology Apollo was the sun god who would fly across the heavens each day in his fiery chariot. Kings throughout history declared that they were direct descendants of the sun. They recognized it as the source of life. The same energy and life force that ancients recognized can be utilized in your space clearing. Fire can bring forth an energy of transformation, purification, and healing.

Here is an exercise to deepen your connection to the fire element:

1. Sit still and quiet your mind.
2. Light a candle and gaze steadily into the flame.
3. Feel the warmth of the candle. Imagine that the warmth of the flame is filling you.
4. Expand your awareness and imagine that you become the sun. Feel the warmth of the sun fill you and radiate from you.
5. Visualize the Spirit of Fire filling you. Like the great phoenix in flight, let the power and beauty of fire fill you. There is enormous beauty in fire. Fire can be a single candle flame in a monastery or the purple and orange conflagration of a sky at sunset. It is the icy fire of a shooting star in the heavens, but it is also the gentle warmth of the sun in a summer meadow. Feel and find the part of you that dwells in the

understanding of fire. For some, connecting with the energy of fire is a physical sensation. They might feel a surge of warmth travel through the body. Connect with the fire that dwells in your mind and soul, and your clearing ceremonies will be powerful and brilliant.

6. Give thanks for the Spirit of Fire.

CONNECTING WITH THE SPIRIT OF AIR

Air is sound. Air is oxygen. Air is life. With every breath you take, you are inhaling air that has been in every nook and cranny of our world, from the dry air of the Sahara to the peaks of the Himalayas, to the lush and humid rain forests. Our atmosphere contians argon atoms, which disperse so rapidly that the air you breathe now will contain at least 15 of the exact same argon atoms that you breathed one year ago. The breath that you just took contained at least 400,000 of the same argon atoms that Gandhi breathed throughout his life. Shakespeare inhaled some of the same atoms that you just breathed, as did Plato and Geronimo. Air is the unifying force in the world. Thus, aligning with the Spirit of Air in your space clearing is a powerful way to connect more deeply with the world.

Here is an exercise to deepen your connection to the air element:

1. Sit still and quiet your mind.

2. Begin by inhaling and sensing the air within you and around you. Imagine that you are aware of the oxygen flowing through your body. Feel the feeling of the air as it touches your face, surrounds your hands, and envelopes your entire body.

3. Take a deep breath and imagine that you are aware of your body absorbing the air and how it sustains your body.

4.   Expand your awareness until you can sense that the air inside of you is connected with the air flowing around our planet.

5.   Now expand your awareness even more so that you feel oneness with clouds, winds, and the vast expanse of the sky.

6.   Continue until you imagine that you have become the Spirit of Air. Imagine that you are now the soft morning breeze that comes in the night, you are a seagull spiraling higher and higher in the crystal-blue sky, you are the wind howling through a pine tree on a cold winter night, you are a baby's breath.

7.   The more you connect with and "call" the Spirit of Air into yourself, the more the Spirit of Air will fill your home.

8.   Give thanks for the Spirit of Air.

CHAPTER 8

Holy Water

One of the most powerful tools for cleansing the spirit of a house, a room, or any personal space is water. It can cleanse and purify a house of negative, stagnant energy and restore to it a feeling of clarity and peace. Water is a conductor of energy and has innate purifying properties. It has been used in spiritual ceremonies and has been linked to the mysteries of human existence throughout history.

In ancient times, water was treasure itself. Communities grew around rivers... the river was the lifeblood of the community. Wells and fountains formed the center axis for the town or hamlet. It was at the well or fountain where women would gather to do their cleaning, but more importantly, it was the water that formed a nexus of cohesion for the community. Stories were shared; strategies for facing the challenges of life were discussed. In some unseen, yet potent way, the water was the catalyst for the building of community and the bridging of cultures. Even in nomadic desert communities, waterholes were gathering places where information was disseminated and wisdom was garnered.

Water was so important to the cohesion of a culture that some societies worshipped the spirits of the water and felt that some waters had healing properties. The Egyptians, Persians, Indians, and Greeks all had deities associated with wells, fountains, or streams. In Europe and Britain, pagans worshipped at sacred springs. In France, the cathedrals of Chartres and Nîmes were built over the springs that were the center point of worship in pre-Christian times. To this day, the water at Lourdes in France is thought to have healing properties. In England, York Minster, Carlisle Cathedral, and Glastonbury were built over sacred pagan springs. In Ireland, St. Patrick chose sacred well sites for his churches.

Throughout history, water has represented purification and cleansing. Legends about great purifying floods have always been a part of historical lore. The best known is the biblical story of Noah. But the ancient Sumerians had a similar legend, as did the Greeks, who believed Zeus purified the harmful ways of humans with a great deluge. Similarly, purifying flood stories can be found in the Native American culture, and in other cultures around the world.

On an individual level, this power of purification is represented by the sacrament of baptism. Although baptism is usually associated with Christianity, many cultures throughout time used water for spiritual purification. This can be seen most acutely in the reverence for the Ganges, India's holy river, which serves as an arterial waterway bringing symbolic purification to millions. Every day, Hindu pilgrims bathe in the river to spiritually cleanse and purify themselves. Some Buddhist temples also have places for ceremonial ablution. In Islamic tradition, ritual acts of ablution are performed using water outside the mosque.

CREATION OF HOLY WATER FOR SPACE CLEARING

Holy water is a purveyor of a mysterious force—an emissary for the power of the Creator. It isn't just a symbol of cleansing and purity; it actually contains sacred life-force energy. Holy water can powerfully and instantly cleanse negative energy and call forth blessings and protection.

Long recognized for its amazing powers for renewal and transformation, in cultures around the world, holy water has been used in space clearing ceremonies. Even in modern times, the spiritual cleansing properties of water are still recognized. For example, in Catholic churches, a font near the front door is filled with holy water for people entering to dip their fingers into before blessing themselves. Some Catholics will flick holy water over a person or space as a blessing or a way of consecrating the energy there.

You can obtain holy water from a shrine or temple, or you can create holy water. The potency of your holy water will vary with the source of the water, how it is made, and who makes it. The more sacred the stream or the place from which it is obtained, the greater the water's strength. For example, water obtained from the Chalice

Well in Glastonbury has wonderful and unique qualities. Additionally, the more powerful the intent, prayers, and mantras used when preparing the water, the more hallowed and healing it becomes. And, most important, the more spiritually attuned the person who blesses it, the greater the sanctity of the water.

You can make excellent holy water for your space clearing, if you prepare it carefully and lovingly. If possible, obtain your water from a natural source, such as a freshwater spring or from rainwater, which carries the lofty energy of the heavens. These are some of the very best places to obtain water for space clearing as the water comes directly from the depths of Mother Earth or from the bounty of Father Sky. (If you use rainwater, wait until it has been raining for a while, as the pollutants in the air will be present in the first hour of the rain.) You can also use water from a body of water such as a lake or the ocean.

However, since many of us do not have easy access to fresh water from these sources, you can use water that has been bottled. Any natural spring water that you purchase that says "bottled at source" can be used. It is better if the water you purchase comes in glass bottles rather than plastic. Also, it is useful to note where the water came from, as it will retain energy imprints of this place. If you have no other water, then it's all right to use tap water.

"Charging" Water

Once you have obtained your water, you will want to "charge" it to infuse it with robust energy before using it for clearing. Charging water is like charging your car's batteries. You are infusing the water with energy.

Water gathered directly from a spring, seawater, or rainwater does not always need to be charged, because it still has the vibrant energy of the natural world in its essence. Some lake water does not need to be charged, yet others do. (Use your intuition on a case by case basis.)

Bottled water and especially tap water need to be renewed. Water that has been sitting in a plastic container in a grocery store—or has come from a tap and has been chlorinated, fluorinated, and filtered—has lost its vibrancy and spirit.

You can do this in the ways outlined in the following section. All the methods are effective; the method you use depends on the project you have at hand. Bear in mind that water used for space clearing should be put in a glass or ceramic bowl, as metals and plastic can influence the energy of the water.

Prayers and Mantras to Charge Water

The most important aspect of energizing water is done through your prayers and reverence. Holding your right hand over the container of water, with your left hand held upward, palm facing the heavens, imagine light entering into your left and pouring out of your right hand into the water. As you do this, add your prayers or mantras that the water be made sacred. This should be done in the early morning when the earth energy is freshest.

Continue until you feel that the water has been saturated with Spirit. Know that every molecule of the water is now infused with the power of your prayers and your intention, and that whatever this water touches will be transformed.

Holy water needs to be treated with respect. It must be put in a clean container that has only been used for holy water. It is best to purchase a container for this purpose; however, you may use any glass or ceramic container or bowl that has been thoroughly cleaned and dedicated for use for holy water. It should be stored in a place of honor, such as on your home altar, and handled with respect.

Solar-Charged Water

Take the water that you plan on using for your ceremony and place it in a bowl. A ceramic or glass bowl is better than metal, unless you have some specific purpose in mind that requires infusing the metal's energy into the water. For example, you could use a copper bowl to infuse water with the expansive energy of copper.

Leave your bowl in the morning sunlight where it can soak up the healing properties of solar energy. Make sure the rays of light actually penetrate the surface of the water. The bowl needs to be left outside rather than next to a sunny closed window. Usually about three hours is sufficient for the water to become solar charged.

Solar water is great to use in dark rooms or rooms that feel like they have a dark or heavy energy. It's also good to use in a room where someone has been ill. Solar water has a very yang, exuberant, sociable energy. It is wonderful to use when you want to add life and vigor to any environment.

Lunar-Charged Water

Leave your bowl of water outdoors on a clear moonlit night in order to infuse it with lunar essence. Moon water has a wonderful feminine healing aspect and can contribute to softening energy in a room.

This is particularly good in a room where intense emotions such as anger or sadness have been felt. Lunar-charged water has a very gentle, healing nature that makes it particularly useful for clearing after illness. It is also excellent for creating a restful energy in bedrooms and places of meditation. It is conducive to good dreams and incubating creative ideas.

Starlight Water

Leaving water out to absorb energy from the stars on a clear night will give it a very special energy that is full of joy and magic. Star energy is at its most intense on nights with no moon or very little moon. The water that is instilled with star energy is wonderful for helping make dreams come true and bringing more rapture into life.

Spiraled Water

Spiraling water strengthens its energy. Hold the water in your container and spiral it round and round. You can twirl the container, or use a clean finger, a wooden spoon, or a stick to spiral it. This potentizes the water.

Water flowing in nature naturally moves in spiraling patterns. These spiral movements replenish the water's energy and increase its electromagnetic current. Still water or water flowing out of straight pipes does not have this vital essence, but you can restore it by gently swirling it.

Prayer Water

Hold your hands over the water and imagine that energy from the universe is flowing to and through you into the water. You can say a prayer for the water to be infused with Spirit, or you can imagine a rainbow of light cascading from your hands into the water. You can also chant over the water.

Additionally, you can write empowering words or a prayer and place the water bowl on top of these written words or attach them to the bowl or jar. Cleansed blessed crystals or special stones can also be placed in the water to energize it.

Rainbow Water

It is not always easy to find three hours of sunlight or moonlight if the weather is overcast. And sometimes the winter temperatures will freeze any water that you leave outside. So here is a technique to "charge water" on overcast days or winter days. I learned this method from my Hawaiian kahuna teacher 45 years ago.

According to traditional Hawaiian beliefs, rainbows are gifts from the gods and water is holy. It is used for blessing and healing ceremonies. You can use this ancient Hawaiian shamanic technique for the purifying and energizing of water.

Take your hand and place it palm down over the container of water that you are going to use for your ceremony. Do not touch the water, but slowly move your hand in a circular, clockwise motion over the surface. While you do this, imagine a cascade of rainbows coming out of your hand, radiating the water with serenity and joy.

Crystal-Charged Water

Stones and crystals can powerfully energize water. Simply place your quartz crystals, which you have cleansed and blessed, into the water for at least 24 hours. This method works especially well if you can place the container in a window where light can penetrate the crystal—the light helps activate the crystal.

The stones in the quartz family, such as rose quartz, amethyst, citrine, or smoky quartz, are excellent. You can also use any stone that you desire to transfer its energy into the water. See Appendix B for a list of stones and crystals and their qualities.

This water is excellent to use in a healing room in the home. This Crystal Water is also good for watering and misting indoor plants.

Warning: Do not drink the water in which you have soaked stones, unless you are sure of the safety of the stone in the water, as some stones contain lead, arsenic, or mercury.

Flower Water

Simply floating a flower or flower petals in water can infuse the subtle energies of those flowers into the water. As a suggestion, use flowers that you know are not coated in pesticides. Natural is best.

If you put your water with the flowers floating on it either in the sunshine or in the moonlight, the water becomes even more infused with the flower's energies. You can remove the petals and flowers and the water will still have their energy You can also use herbs such as rosemary or lemon verbena. Refer to Appendix C for suggestions of flowers you might choose.

Flower Essences to Empower Holy Water

Flower essences contain the pure spiritual essence of each individual flower. They are created by picking a flower at its peak in the early morning hours and floating it in pure spring water while the sun shines on it. This is done in a meditative state to invite the energy of the flower into the water.

Flower essences are great for shifting the energy fields in a home. They can uplift the energy in an environment and create an energy network, like a delicate gossamer weaving, that is interlaced throughout a space. A space that has been misted with flower essence literally shines with a webbing of etheric light.

The flower essences you use will depend on the kind of energy you want to create. For a partial list of essences and their qualities, see Appendix C. The following lists of recommended essences will also help get you started:

- *To bring calmness and peace into a home:* chamomile, centaury, cherry plum, lavender, mimulus, water violet

- *To awaken mental clarity and focus in a home:* blackberry, cerato, clematis, peppermint, rosemary, Shasta daisy

- *To cleanse old patterns out of a home (such as after a divorce or trauma):* Bach's Rescue Remedy blend, cayenne, fireweed, gorse, sagebrush, star of Bethlehem

- *To create a protective shield around a home:* garlic, pennyroyal, yarrow

- *To ignite energy and vitality:* Indian paintbrush, morning glory, peppermint, wild rose

- *To summon spiritual awakening:* angel's trumpet, angelica, black-eyed Susan, iris, lotus

Creating Your Own Flower Essences for Your Home

Some of the highest-quality vibrational flower essences are those that have been created by people who have dedicated their life to this work. They usually have a highly attuned ability to sense the energy of the plant and assist the infusion of the flower's energy into the water. Bach Flower Remedies, Californian Flower Essences, Australian Bush Flower Essences, and Alaskan Essences are all companies of good reputation. I particularly like the flower and environmental essences from Alaskan Essences; they come from wonderfully clean air and unpolluted land, and the integrity and attunement of the owners is remarkable. The powerful yet subtle way that the owners work with the flower energy is impeccable.

However, there are times when you might want to create your own flower essences. It can be exhilarating to participate in this process. Here are the steps and considerations for making your own flower essences:

- *Type of water:* Use spring water only, either from a local spring or store-bought water that is bottled at the source.

- *Types of flowers:* Obtain a book about the various qualities of individual flowers, or you can use your intuition to find the flower that feels best for you.

- *Picking the flowers:* Plants must be at their best (not treated with chemicals) and, if possible, wild and picked at a peak of vibrancy. Collect in the early morning when there is still dew on the plant. Some dew is condensation, but some of the fluid in the dew actually comes out of the plant, so the dew has an energy imprint of the plant. (Dew is transpiration, not only condensation. When you make an essence, you are re-creating dew.) It's important to ask for the plant's permission. And once given, say a blessing of gratitude or leave a gift, such as a strand of hair or cornmeal. I know some Native Americans who leaves coins as a gift. The gift is less important than the love that comes with it.

- *Floating the flowers:* At sunrise, float the flowers in a bowl filled with your spring water, and do not submerge. When the flowers float, they act as filters for the sunlight into the water.

- *Timing:* You can tell the moment that the energy of the plant has been released into the water—it may take an hour or even two hours. Sometimes (rarely) it can take just half an hour. The flower will seem a little less vibrant . . . as its life force has gone into the water. Once the flower energy has entered the water, filter the water through a very clean cloth such as cheesecloth or a clean dish towel.

- *Give the plants back to the earth:* Give thanks for the giveaway of the plant or flower, and carefully give it back to the earth.

- *Mother Tincture:* This tincture is a highly concentrated form of your essence. Take a very clean glass bottle and fill it with ½ spring water and ½ brandy. The brandy should be French brandy or any high-quality brandy. This creates what is called the "Mother Tincture." This is your concentrated stock from which you can make bottles of your flower essence. If you are going to use it immediately, then you can use the water without brandy. The brandy is necessary as a preservative, so the water doesn't mold over time and it preserves the essence of the flower as well.

- *Your stock bottle:* Two drops of your Mother Tincture into 1 ounce (30 ml) or 7 drops in 2 ounces (50 ml) in a clean glass bottle of ½ brandy and ½ spring water. This creates your stock bottle. This is what you use in your work.

- *Misting your home:* From your stock bottle, put three drops in water with 25 percent brandy (or more or less if you desire) into a mister. (Glass misters are best.) You can then use this to mist your home. Your entire home will sing with energy and light as a result. Flower essences are subtle, yet powerful. (See the following section for more information on misting your home.)

- *Spiraling the water:* To increase the potency of your flower essences for your home, you can first spiral the water one way, then spiral it the other way (or alternatively, you can swirl it in a figure-eight motion). The spiraling movement increases the energy and potency of the water. (Refer to section on Spiraled Water on page 130.)

SPACE CLEARING METHODS USING WATER

As you begin your clearing, you may want to invoke the Spirit of Water to help you in your work. To do this, place a bowl of holy water on your Blessing Altar. Take a few moments to still your mind and fully connect with the Spirit of Water. Imagine a beautiful cascade of mountain water flowing down steep stones to an alpine valley full of delicate wildflowers. This calls upon the Spirit of Water to bring the renewing energy of a cascading waterfall into your space clearing.

Clearing a Room by Flicking Water

One way to use holy water for space clearing is to dip a leaf, flower, or small branch into the water, then flick it into the space.

In some ancient traditions, the shaman would carry a bowl of water in one hand. With his other hand, he carried a branch of herbs or a small sprig from an evergreen tree or a flower. He would dip this into the consecrated water and vigorously flick the end of the branch around the room, so that small drops of water were dispersed throughout the air.

To use this method of space clearing, walk around the periphery of the room. Wherever you sense energy that is stagnant or negative, dip your small twig, flower, or stem into the water and lightly but firmly flick the water into the area. (A twig of rosemary is excellent to use because of its purifying qualities.) If energy is really stuck, then flick the branch seven times, wait a moment to sense if the energy has cleared, and if not, then flick seven times again.

This method of flicking seven times is traditional in many cultures. You do not need to saturate an area; a few drops are enough. (Be careful not to get water drops on fine furniture or anywhere it will stain.)

If you are clearing an area that has very delicate energy, such as a nursery for a newborn baby or very young child, you might want to use a flower for flicking the water. In this case, you would use much gentler, softer movements of the wrist so as not to damage the flower or disturb the delicate protective web of energy you want to weave in such a situation.

Flowers are sometimes used to establish fresh, new energy after a room has already been cleared with a stronger purifying tool such as a pine twig.

Here is a partial list of some options you can try. You can also use your intuition to discover others.

- *Pine branch:* Excellent for clearing very heavy or negative energy. Extremely purifying and cleansing. Good for clearing after illness or depression, or when someone is feeling stuck in their life.

- *Cedar branch:* Some of the same positive aspects as pine, but somewhat softer in energy. Excellent for clearing spiritual energies.

- *Lemon verbena branch:* Excellent for shifting the energy in a room quickly and for clearing negative energy following an argument. Increases mental clarity and perception. Leaves a vibrant, refreshing energy.

- *Rosemary:* Purifying and revitalizing, vibrant and emotionally warming.

- *Rose flower:* Good for working with very gentle energy, and for creating a delicate haven of love and affection.

- *Daisy flower:* Especially good for clearing children's rooms and rooms devoted to sociability. A delicate tool best used to create environments filled with joy.

- *Marigold:* These flowers are often used for sacred-water flicking in India. They invite expanding blessings and love.

It is also possible to clear a room using your fingers to gently flick the water throughout the area. Doing this feels very different from using a plant. You may receive energy vibrations as the water leaves your fingers that will help you to decide exactly which areas of the room you need to concentrate on. You don't need to use a lot of water. Even just a drop can be potent.

Misting a Room for Purification

Misting a room will instantly clear out stagnant, emotional energies that have accumulated there.

Emotional energy tends to stagnate in a room long after the events that gave birth to the emotions have passed. After an argument, the air in a room might seem thick and almost charged. This is, in fact, precisely the case. There is an electric "charge" left hanging in the air as a residue from all the negative emotions. This is because negative emotions actually leave a kind of electrical charge hanging in the air.

The fastest way to neutralize this residual energy is to mist the room. Spraying a home with water to create sacred space is one of the simplest and most effective techniques for shifting a home's energy and to cleanse residual emotions.

Misting not only neutralizes emotional charge in a room almost instantly, but also it creates a special negative-ion-rich environment. (The word *negative* doesn't refer to less than positive feelings; it is the term for a particular kind of electrical charge that is beneficial.)

A negative-ion-rich environment is the same environment that you will find next to a waterfall, by the sea, or in a pine forest. Misting is a way of re-creating these refreshing environments through space clearing. When you are in a negative-ion-rich environment, you feel uplifted, alert, and revitalized. In a positive-ion-rich environment, you will feel sluggish and lethargic.

When choosing a water spritzer to use for misting, the finer the spray created, the better. It is best to fill the bottle with spring water. However, if you do not have access to any water other than tap water, then you can "charge" the tap water using the previously suggested methods.

There are many small, beautiful bottles that can be obtained that work very well. (The beauty of the mister is actually an important adjunct to its function, because it helps to consecrate the ritual.) Select one that is comfortable to hold and has an easy-to-use spray mechanism.

The key is to lightly spray all over your room. Don't soak everything. Just send light little puffs of moisture into the air everywhere. You should instantly feel the difference in the room after you have misted. (Plants will also benefit from the regular use of a fine mister.)

The solution you use for misting in space clearing is directly related to your intention. You can add a few drops of a flower essence (or even a small amount of essential oil) to the charged water in your bottle. The ones you use will be a determining factor in the results you gain, so consider carefully.

But don't feel overwhelmed. Your intuition is often more valuable than extensive knowledge. Just let go and trust that you will be drawn to exactly the best essences or essential oils for a particular clearing.

As with the flicking method, you will circle each room in a clockwise motion with your mister. Again, don't soak everything. Just send light puffs of mist into the air wherever you sense that the energy needs clearing. Misting is particularly useful for situations where negative emotions are at the heart of what is wrong with the energy. Doing this kind of clearing produces immediate results. The room will feel lighter, fresher, clearer, and much more positive.

Purification Bowl

You can use this method in conjunction with any other clearing method you are using and for every kind of room clearing. Before you begin a space clearing ceremony, take a bowl of "charged" water and place it in the center of the room that you are clearing. Hold the intention in your mind that this water will absorb stagnant energy that is released during the ceremony.

If you have very dense energy to clear in a room, add a small amount of sea salt to the "charged" water. When the ceremony is complete, carefully take the water and pour it down a drain. Run clear cold water afterward for 30 seconds. Sometimes after a very intense clearing, the water will actually look murky and dull. Clean the water container out with cold water and allow it to air dry or, if possible, to dry in the sun.

BATHING FOLLOWING THE SPACE CLEARING

It is valuable to complete your space clearing with an aura clearing of yourself and all the household inhabitants. Clearing a home without also resetting the energy of the people who live there is like washing all of your clothes, but then forgetting to bathe your body! Using water for clearing the energy of the people who live in a space especially helps them to attune to the home's new energies.

After you have finished your clearing, all members of the household should take (salt) baths or shower before they go to bed. (A few drops of rosemary essential oil or rosemary bath oil are alternatives to salt.) Explain to them that as they bathe, they can visualize the new, fresh energy flowing through their homes. Tell them that they will emerge from their bath cleansed and re-vitalized and fully in tune with this new energy. If a bath is not available, then briskly rubbing salt on the body while showering can produce the same effect. After the bath or shower, a cold rinse is recommended.

SPIRIT OF WATER

Using water for cleansing your home and having "charged" water within your home calls forth the living Spirit of Water. This is important, for we are in constant inter-relationship with the Spirit of Water through the waters of life that course through our veins. Water makes up the greater part of our physical bodies. You can go for long periods of time without eating, but if you stop drinking water, your body will not survive.

Every beat of your heart connects you to the universal Spirit of Water, which links you to the waters of our entire planet. The water that you drink and the water that flows through your body is the same water that was, at one time in the evolution of the planet, frozen high on the snowcapped mountains. The water within you was once cascading down mountain streams to the sea below. The water inside you has been high in a cloud mass above the earth, has fallen as soft gentle rain, and has seen the bottom of the deep sea. The water that runs through your body has ebbed through the bodies of your ancestors and will flow through the bodies of your descendants.

The power of the Spirit of Water is intuition and emotion and spirituality. It is renewal and rebirth. It is soothing cool showers on a sultry afternoon. Water heals, cleanses, and rejuvenates. From a gentle mist to a summer's rain to a raging thunderstorm, water cleanses all that it encompasses. Water Spirit resides in a still mountain pond; it is in the oasis pool in the desert where wild animals are drawn to life-giving waters; it is in the majestic sea where dolphins leap and whales swim deep. Water can be included as a powerful ingredient in any preparation for energy clearing. If you choose to use water in your preparation process, it is important to tune in to the Spirit of Water within you, as well as to physically cleanse yourself with water before your clearing ceremony.

Connecting with the Spirit of Water

1. Sit still and quiet your mind.

2. Begin by feeling the water within you and around you. Imagine that you are aware of the waters flowing through your body. Notice the moisture in your skin, your mouth, and your eyes. Feel how the moisture in the air touches your face, surrounds your hands, and envelopes your entire body.

3. Drink a glass of water and imagine that you are aware of how your body absorbs the water and how the water sustains and hydrates your body.

4. Expand your awareness until you can sense that the water you are drinking and the water within you is part of the water flowing in streams and rivers.

5. Now expand your awareness even more so that you feel oneness with all lakes and the vast expanse of all seas.

6. Continue until you imagine that you have become the Spirit of Water. Imagine that you are now the tiny dew drops that come in the night, you are a dolphin splashing and dancing in the crystal-blue sea, you are a drop of rain, you are a mountain waterfall.

7. The more you connect with and "call" the Spirit of Water into yourself, the more the Spirit of Water will fill your home.

8. Give thanks for the Spirit of Water.

CHAPTER 9

Healing Earth

Viewed from outer space, Earth shines like a beautiful blue jewel set against a sea of jet-black darkness. The swirling clouds of her delicate atmosphere drift in spirals of white, marking the blue orb like delicate veins on marble. The wonders of our precious planet were intuitively sensed by our ancestors, who worshipped our planet as the Mother Goddess, the foundation of life.

When you connect with the Spirit of the Earth in your space clearing, you are grounding your home into a primeval and powerful force for healing. The passage of the seasons and the daily rhythms of our lives are all in accordance with the cycles of the Earth. Mother Earth's soil, her forests, her rocks and mountains, and her plains and vegetation are the bounty that nourishes us, body and soul.

SALT FOR SPACE CLEARING

Salt is a gift from the earth that has special significance for space clearing. It has been known throughout time for its remarkable purifying properties. In the ocean, salt acts as an antiseptic to destroy bacteria. The ancient practice of tossing salt over the left shoulder to avert bad luck is based on the traditional use of salt to dispel negative energy. Because of its unique virtues, salt is one of the most essential elements in your repertoire of space clearing tools.

In performing purification for your own home, it is best to obtain natural salt, either sea salt or rock salt, which has not been iodized. Which one you choose will depend on your overall intention for the clearing.

Sea salt will call forth the powers of the sea, which are especially conducive to cleansing and emotional healing. Rock salt, on the other hand, is associated with the powers of the earth, and is very useful for achieving a sense of balance and grounding. These differences are very subtle, so use of either kind of salt will have a similar effect overall.

Salt Purification for Your Home

There are several ways you can use salt in a space clearing ceremony. Placing a bowl of salt on your Blessing Altar while you are space clearing will help to ground and neutralize any negative energy you encounter as you work.

You can also take a small bowl of salt and place it in the center of each room while you are clearing it. Or you can sprinkle salt throughout each room. Pay particular attention to the corners, where stagnant energy tends to gather.

Salt sprinkled during a clearing should be left for 24 hours before being swept up in order to allow enough time for it to absorb all of the negative energy. And salt used in space clearing should *never* be eaten. It should be used only once and then rinsed down the sink followed by plenty of cold running water.

Salt, Rice, and Ash

A traditional Eastern way to use salt for space clearing is to mix it with equal parts of rice to toss throughout a space.

Additionally, in some traditions it has sacred ash mixed into it. Calligraphy and blessings are written on paper and then ceremonially burned and added to the rice-salt mixture. The ash contains the essence of the prayers. You may want to write your prayers and blessings on a piece of paper, burn it, and then mix the ashes with your rice and salt. (After 24 hours it can be swept up or vacuumed.)

CRYSTALS FOR SPACE CLEARING

Clear quartz crystal, another gift from the earth, is composed of silicon dioxide. Like salt, quartz is one of the earth's most common and plentiful minerals. Used in space clearing, quartz crystals can act as generators of energy. Because crystals can act as catalysts for human consciousness, they possess the ability to distill, magnify, and transmit your intention into a room.

By placing a quartz crystal on your Blessing Altar, you will be able to deepen and radiate the energy field that you have created there. Natural faceted crystals can also be used as "wands" to implant sacred symbols into a room or to direct energy. To do this, hold an intention of a particular sacred symbol or ideal in your mind while directing the crystal toward a particular place in a room. (You can even outline the symbol in the air with the wand.)

Cleansing Your Space Clearing Crystals

Regularly cleansing your clear quartz will keep it vitalized. This should be done after every clearing, or it will eventually lose its vibrancy.

There are several ways to cleanse your crystals. Also see the box "Simple Cleansing Techniques for Your Tools" on page 39.

1. *Solar Cleansing:* Place your crystal where the rays of the sun will directly fall on it. Leave it there for three to four hours. Then wrap it in black or dark purple silk to keep the energy intact.

2. *Saltwater Cleansing:* Combine at least 1 cup of water with ½ cup of salt in a nonplastic, nonmetal container. (Glass is best.) Embed your crystal in the salt before it begins to dissolve, and let it soak in the solution for at least 24 hours. You can also cover your crystal in salt without the water to cleanse it. (The less processed the salt the better.)

3. *Eucalyptus Oil Cleansing:* Holding your crystal in your hand, rub eucalyptus oil over its entire surface. As you apply the oil, begin at the base (this will be the bottom or flat surface of the crystal) and work up to the top facet (the tip or apex of the crystal where all sides come together).

SACRED DANCE FOR SPACE CLEARING

Dance is an ancient way of celebrating our connection to the earth. As the feet touch the ground, the body reaches for the heavens, thus establishing a sacred link between Mother Earth and Grandfather Sky. Your body can be one of the most exquisite and wondrous tools for space clearing. It can become your holy instrument to channel energy and light into a space.

Tai chi or yoga classes can help you learn to use your body in a graceful way for channeling energy, but it is not necessary to do so. These kind of classes can help you to get in touch with your physical form and understand how to sense and respond to energy with your body, but you can also experiment on your own, using your intuition to find those poses and movements that are most expressive of Spirit for you.

To clear a space using your body, begin by standing at the entrance with your hands in the prayer position (palms together and held near your chest with fingers pointed up).

Take a deep breath and exhale. Allow your awareness to expand so that you feel that you are filling every part of the room.

Step beyond your mind and all linear thought processes. Slowly allow your "body wisdom" to take over and begin to dance.

Move, sway, shake, flow. Let your hands, arms, body, and heart take over.

You might find your arms moving in a spontaneous spiraling movement in one area and a soft pushing motion in another.

Let your body become a sacred vessel for universal awareness to surge through the room.

When you sense that the energy in the room is balanced and complete, draw the sign of infinity (a horizontal figure eight) in the air to seal the energy of the room.

It's all right to use music as you do this; however, as a suggestion, house your music in something ceremonial.

PENDULUMS AND DOWSING FOR SPACE CLEARING

The art of dowsing has been used for thousands of years for indicating energy fields. Prehistoric rock paintings in Algeria depict early dowsers, and research has uncovered evidence suggesting that the ancient Chinese and Egyptians used dowsing. The first written descriptions of dowsing appeared in the Middle Ages.

Although there are many schools of thought regarding why dowsing is successful, practitioners of this ancient art all agree on one point: it works.

Many dowsers believe that dowsing works because they subconsciously tune in to the stream of wisdom available at the level of the collective unconscious of all people. The dowser receives information from this source, causing muscles to twitch, which in turn causes the pendulum to swing. In other words, the body of the dowser becomes a receiving station to access the energy flows of the space around them. The dowsing tool acts as a focal point, or amplifier, for the information received.

You can use pendulums in your space clearing for clearing energy as well as for detecting energy fields. Any weight attached to the end of a cord or chain can be used for pendulum dowsing. If you are purchasing a pendulum, find one that both looks and feels good to you. Before you begin to work with your pendulum, you will want to energize it. You can do this by holding your hands over it and imagining that light is radiating out of your hands into the pendulum. Energizing your pendulum will almost always improve the way it works for you.

To use your pendulum for space clearing, hold the cord or chain firmly between your thumb and an index finger several inches from the pendulum (a comfortable range is usually between 3 and 12 inches, or 8 to 30 cm), so that it can swing freely and smoothly.

Go throughout each room in your home, allowing the pendulum to swing in small circles. Anywhere that it begins to swing in wider circles or won't spin at all can indicate the need for clearing.

The movement indicates that energy is too active (swinging wildly) or very stagnant (not moving at all).

Allow the pendulum to spiral in that area until it begins to swing in small, even circles again. This is an indication that the energy in that area has been cleared. (You can program the pendulum to respond differently if larger and smaller spirals don't work for you. Some people prefer back and forth rather than circles.)

Since the beginning of time, people have used symbols to express feelings of connection to Spirit, to the earth, and to the multitude of life around us. Because these symbols have been found throughout the ages and across many cultures, I believe that they come to us from the energy of the earth. They are the earth speaking through us, healing us, and uniting us with all of nature.

You can implant the energy of a mystic symbol in a room, thus sealing the energy that you have created there. You can do this by either outlining the symbol in the air with your fingers or a wand or by visualizing it.

When using your fingers, use your index finger and middle finger together. You can also draw the outlines of the symbol in the air using an elongated crystal or a wooden wand (or any kind of wand that feels right to you). This will further imprint the energy of the symbol in the atmosphere of the environment.

Any symbol that has significance for you can be effectively used to seal the energy of a room. Reiki practitioners use Reiki symbols, for instance. Use your intuition to find which symbols are best for you. The following list outlines intended purposes and the symbols that work for them:

- *Expanding the energy in a room:* Make a spiral starting at the center and working outward. (You can do this with your wand upright or pointing outward.)

- *Protecting the energy in a room:* The Cross, the five-pointed star (pentagram), and the six-pointed star (Seal of Solomon) are all excellent symbols to use.

- *Closing the circle of energy:* Make a circle on each of the four walls, saying, "The circle is now complete."

- *Sealing love into a room:* Visualize or draw in the air the shape of a heart. This is a contemporary symbol that is simple but powerful.

- *Grounding and revitalizing a home:* Draw a tree in the air, complete with roots and branches. By doing this you are planting the energy of the sacred Tree of Life into the home such that this symbol continues to ground and replenish the home energy.

CONNECTING WITH THE SPIRIT OF THE EARTH

Our connection with the earth goes back to the beginnings of our history. From our earliest times, humans have had a dynamic relationship with the earth. People saw the world as teeming with life. Every rock, tree, and mountain was alive and had a spirit. The context of human life was firmly rooted in a natural world infused with diversity and spirit. Folklore abounds with stories of human beings emerging from the earth; in some languages, the origins of the word *man* come from "earth born." The Romanian historian Mircea Eliade wrote that, "Even among Europeans today there lingers an obscure feeling of mystical unity with the native earth; and this is not just a sentiment of love for one's country or for the ancestors buried for generations around the village churches." He believed that this sense of connection to earth was a primary part of a human being's psyche, transcending time and culture, and gave people a sense of belonging. When you use any aspect of Earth in your space clearing, you bring forward the energy of a living, conscious planet.

To connect with the Spirit of the Earth:

1. Sit still and quiet your mind.

2. Begin by feeling the earth within you and around you. The food in your body has come from the earth. At the end of your days your body returns to the earth. Imagine that you are aware of your body's connection to the earth.

3. Slowly eat something that was grown in the earth, such as a carrot. Become fully aware of the food entering your body and how your body absorbs the nutrients.

4. Expand your awareness until you can sense that the earth inside of you is part of all the earth, mountains, hills, canyons, and green valleys.

5. Now expand your awareness even more so that you feel oneness with our beautiful Mother Earth.

6. Continue until you imagine that you have become the Spirit of the Earth. Imagine that you are a mountain peak; you are an ancient oak tree; you are a vast desert under the stars; you are a moss-covered forest.

7. The more you connect with and call the Spirit of the Earth into yourself, the more the Spirit will fill your life.

8. Give thanks for the Spirit of the Earth.

THE VIBRATIONAL FREQUENCIES OF PLANTS

Elemental Space Clearing works with the physical and etheric properties of plants, especially in the concentrated form of essential oils. (You'll learn more about Elemental Space Clearing in the next chapter, including how to combine essential oils with mudras to do powerful and potent space clearings.)

Essential oils are different from flower essences, as they are an actual extract of the plant or flower (extracted through distillation with steam or cold pressing); flower essences are derived from the vibration of the plant.

In ancient times, plant and flower essential oils were used by shamans, priests, and priestesses of almost every spiritual and religious tradition throughout the world. These special oils were thought to dispel negative energies, banish "evil," purify temples and sacred places, and invite gods and goddesses to bless a space. The smoke or aroma of plants was also thought to help with communication and communion with spiritual realms.

Modern research is discovering what these ancient people knew: the scent of various plants and flower oils affect the way we feel—sometimes dramatically so. (See Appendix C for more specific information.)

Every plant and flower has its own innate and individual qualities that can be used to shift the energy and feeling of a space. In the Elemental Space Clearing work that you do, carefully choose the essential oils that you use. Align the intention for the space with the properties of the oil.

For example, if the members of a household have been in a stagnant cycle, you might want to use stimulating oils such as rosemary, peppermint, lemon, or fir needle in conjunction with the mudras. If a person is feeling agitated and irritated, then you might want to use oils that are more soothing such as lavender, rose, or neroli.

CONNECTING WITH THE PLANT OVERSOUL

To powerfully and profoundly expand the benefit of using essential oils, it's valuable to connect with the oversoul of each plant or flower that you are using. (You will be doing this during the first stage, preparation.) For example, the "lavender oversoul" is the residing and connecting spirit that oversees and connects all lavender plants. A single lavender bush is just one fragment of the residing whole.

When you connect with the lavender oversoul, you are inviting the energy of the whole to be present. It is essential that when you form this communication link, you offer thanks and gratitude. When you do this there is a subtle but remarkable energy shift as the oil you use becomes potentized and much, much more powerful in its effect on a space or a home.

Visualize the Plant Oversoul

To start, simply imagine the plant that you are using in its natural environment. For example, if you are going to use a lemon essential oil, you might imagine a lemon tree on a high plateau in Spain. Its leaves are a dark, shiny green, and the lemons look like orbs of light in the sun.

Connect in such a way that you feel that you are shape-shifting to become the tree. You can feel the sun above; you can feel the cool earth beneath your roots. You can feel your fruit hanging heavy and pregnant on your limbs.

Now expand from this image to images of lemon trees in other areas, maybe trees in northeast India and northern Burma, where they originated, to Italy, Corsica, the Middle East, and to California and Florida.

Continue expanding your perception wider and wider until there is an awareness that you are connected to all lemon trees throughout the world.

Finally, retreat into stillness as you await the arrival of the oversoul.

Note that the oversoul may look like a human, or they may take another form. Sometimes they are simply a light or a sound or a symbol. Accept the form that the oversoul arrives in.

Give thanks to the oversoul. You can also ask for support in your clearing and blessing. This powerfully increases the potency of the oil that you use.

OILS FOR THE FOUR STAGES OF SPACE CLEARING

It is important that anytime you use essential oils for space clearing, you attune with the oversoul of each plant, as this greatly magnifies the power of the oil. Using oils without this attunement doesn't allow the strongest energy to come forward.

Not everyone likes the same oils. Elemental Space Clearing relies heavily on intuition, so you will need to listen to your inner voice to find the right oils for the right place. Here are some suggestions of ways you can use oils:

- *One single oil:* You may use a single oil for all four stages of space clearing. For example, you might use rose oil four times—during preparation, purification, invocation, and protection.

- *Four single oils:* You may also use a different single oil for each stage. (Just make sure that they are harmonious together.) For example, you may use rose geranium for preparation, lemon for purification, rose for the invocation, and bergamot for the preservation.

- *One single blend:* You can also use one blend. For example, you might have an orange-tangerine-peppermint blend that you use for every space clearing stage to uplift the energy.

- *Four different blends:* You may create a different blend for each step. (Just make sure that they are harmonious together.) For example, you might use a blend of:

    Preparation: mandarin, petitgrain, and orange
    Purification: lemon and lemongrass
    Invocation: sandalwood and neroli
    Preservation: jasmine, spruce, and fir

There are multiple uses for the essential oil blends you create, beyond their use during the four stages of space clearing. Consider also using your blends in the following ways:

- *Preparation oil blend:* Use this blend anytime that you want to focus your intention on manifesting something.

- *Purification oil blend:* Use anytime that there are thoughts, emotions, or situations that one desires to purify. It can also be used to purify your energy field after being in a negative environment.

- *Invocation oil blend:* This blend can be used anytime that someone wants to connect to their angels, guides, or the spirit realm. It's also good for sending blessings to another.

- *Preservation oil blend:* This can be used anytime that one desires to create a protective veil or energy field around themselves. This is especially valuable when going into a potentially negative situation, before entering a large crowd of people, or before walking into a fluorescent-lit building.

CHOOSING THE OILS FOR YOUR SPACE CLEARING

In addition to rubbing oils into your hands before doing the mudras or using oils with your general space clearing, you may also want to consider an essential oil burner or a burning stick of natural incense. Refer to Appendix D for a deep dive into the properties of different oils, their aromas, and suggestions for making your own blends.

To inspire you to create your own blends, you might start by choosing one of the following oils as a base, depending on the purpose you intend. Follow your nose and your own intuition as you select complementary oils.

- *Invigorating:* basil, eucalyptus, peppermint, rosemary, or thyme

- *Refreshing:* bergamot, blood orange, lemon, orange, or lemongrass

- *Calming:* chamomile (Roman), clary sage, lavender (fine), Melissa (lemon balm), or neroli

- *Soothing:* chamomile (Roman), lavender (fine), Melissa (lemon balm), or vanilla extract

- *Warming:* fennel, frankincense, or sandalwood

- *Purifying:* lemon, silver fir, tea tree, or thyme

- *Centering:* cedarwood, frankincense, patchouli, rose (Turkish), rose geranium, sandalwood, vetiver, or ylang-ylang

- *Sensual:* jasmine, patchouli, rose geranium, vetiver, or ylang-ylang

The best blends come from your inner wisdom, but here are some examples of combinations:

- *Grounding and centering:* geranium, rose, cypress, and sandalwood

- *Sensuous and warm:* ginger, geranium, lavender, orange, patchouli allspice, and ylang-ylang

- *Cheerful and sunny:* bergamot, neroli, and lemon verbena

- *Refreshing and stimulating:* juniper, fir, spruce, peppermint, and rosemary

- *Optimistic and inspiring:* grapefruit, mandarin, and neroli

CHAPTER 10

Elemental Space Clearing *and* Mystic Mudras

Elemental Space Clearing is a practice I created that provides profound keys to inviting the healing rhythm of the natural world into our homes through our bodies and through our hearts. It includes basic tenets of space clearing, but goes even deeper into the underlying energies affecting a space. It reveals the spiritual possibilities lying dormant in our surroundings, dispels stagnant energy, and calls Spirit into a home or business.

I named this method Elemental Space Clearing because the more you align and connect with the elements of nature around you—air, water, fire, and earth—and the more that these aspects of nature are vibrating inside of you, the more powerful and majestic your clearings can be.

Elemental Space Clearing builds upon the basic space clearing methods discussed in Part I. The four stages remain the same, but you'll also utilize the incredible potency and spiritual energy of mudras in combination with essential oils, resins, and flowers (as well as with the power of prayer and the use of your intention). You learn how to attune yourself to the subtle, yet powerful, vibrations of the etheric plant kingdom to cleanse yourself and your space. With these ceremonies, you can improve energies in your living space and in the spaces of others, creating sanctuaries of inspiration and harmony.

WHEN TO DO ELEMENTAL SPACE CLEARINGS VERSUS REGULAR SPACE CLEARINGS

The best way to decide what type of space cleaning to do and when to do a space clearing is to use your intuition. Simply closing your eyes and asking your spirit guides for advice can give you direction about how best to proceed.

Additionally, you can combine various space clearing tools with the mudras. For example, you might go through the steps of space clearing and use a drum for clearing out stagnant energy, then use one of the dispelling mudras in the space as well.

Consider space clearing anytime you feel the need for:

- Cleansing your auric field, thoughts, relationships, emotions, and all of life's challenges
- Grounding or harmonizing
- Manifesting something in your life
- Calling your angels, guides, ancestors, and spirit helpers
- Protection

THE HISTORY OF MUDRAS

Mudras, which means "seals" or "signs" in Sanskrit, are hand, finger, or body gestures used in many cultures across the world for a variety of purposes, including healing, yoga, and martial arts. Mudras have enjoyed a rich history since their emergence in early Egypt thousands of years ago. Following their early beginnings, the esoteric use of sacred hand gestures swept through the ancient world. They were used in Greece, Persia, India, China, and Japan. Particular hand gestures were used to actualize deep inner states, allowing for an alignment of mind, body, and soul.

Mudra healing gestures are also thought to ensure wellness and prevent disease. They are seen as a more powerful form of communication than the spoken word. They evoke thoughts and feelings, and guide energy flow through the body. Movements and hand gestures in ancient temple dancing, used to elevate higher consciousness, are also attributed to mudras.

Universal Gestures

The mudras you'll learn in this chapter came to me through dreams and my own inner knowing. However, you may recognize certain hand shapes and gestures. Many ancient mudras have been shared among different cultures and time periods, and they continue to be recognized as universal symbols. The following are a couple examples:

- *Veneration mudra (prayer hands position):* Pressing palms together and holding them near chest with fingers pointed up. This is used in Japan as a symbol for respect and worship as well as in India as a greeting. This is also the same gesture used in Christianity for praying.

- *Fear not mudra:* Open hand, palm facing forward and fingers pointed up, arm held close to body. This is a sign of peace, protection, and fearlessness. It is commonly known as a symbol for peaceful intentions. Native Americans have also used it as a friendly greeting.

All mudras begin with your hands in the prayer position. Incidentally, in between the mudras or whenever you feel the need to re-center yourself, you can move your hands back into prayer position. As you do this you're connecting to your heart's center and what's important in life. You are remembering who you are. You're remembering the Creator. You're remembering your focus as being that powerful point between above and below. You're remembering that you are the channel for that creative energy of the universe, for the Creator, God.

ELEMENTAL SPACE CLEARING WITH MUDRAS

Mudras work well in space clearing because through them you can channel energy flows of the universe through your fluid movements. Just as mudras are used to align elements and energy within the body, they can be used to do the same in a space. Combining specific body movements and gestures with specially attuned essential oils creates powerful shifts of energy in a dwelling.

In Elemental Space Clearing, your body becomes your space clearing tool. The mudras you choose work in conjunction with essential oils and your intention and prayers. These graceful movements of your hands will be used to deepen the energy you are creating, and bless and seal the energy in a room during your clearings.

Often when you are "dancing a room" in this process, you will form spontaneous mudras with your arms and hands. Realize that a deep wisdom is filling you at that time and that each hand gesture is calling in a needed energy into the room.

The following pages share the different Elemental Space Clearing mudras, when to use them, and associated essential oils. You can choose one or more of the associated oils to rub on your hands before doing each mudra. You'll learn the 10 dispelling mudras first, then 8 activating mudras. You'll go through the motions of the mudra you choose three to nine times—allow your intuition to guide you as to how long you should do a mudra.

Use dispelling mudras when you want to expel a certain kind of energy. For example, if there has been a lot of sadness in the home, consider using "Lotus Flower to Sun" (page 166). You would first rub into your palms one or more essential oils that helps dispel sadness, referring to the list of recommended oils under the mudra. After rubbing your hands together, inhale the scent of the oil three times. Then do the dispelling mudra in the room or space.

If you want to call forth a certain energy into a home, use an activating mudra. For example, to bring in love, rub an activating oil into your palms such as rose or neroli, take three deep inhales of the scent, and then do the mudra "Light of Sun Illuminates the World" (page 176).

DISPELLING
Mudras

1. DISPEL STAGNANT CHI

Words and feelings associated with stagnant chi: depressed, depression, heavy, can't breathe, lackluster, sluggish, suppressed emotions, inactive, dull, dormant

Mudra: Liquid Flowform

ⓐ Move your hands and arms in a flowing, horizontal figure eight (the infinity sign). (Liquid flowforms purify water by creating thousands of tiny swirls that charge it).

ⓑ Feel a flowing energy surge through you as your body moves.

Essential Oils to Dispel Stagnant Chi

Angelica Root	Cinnamon Leaf	Jasmine	Pepper, Black
Anise	Citronella	Juniper	Peppermint
Basil	Clementine	Lavender	Petitgrain
Bay Laurel	Eucalyptus	Lemon	Rose
Blood Orange	Fir, Douglas	Lemongrass	Rosemary
Cajeput	Frankincense	Lemon Verbena	Savory
Cardamom	Ginger	Lime	Tea Tree
Chamomile, Roman	Grapefruit	Neroli Absolute	Thyme
Cedarwood	Hyssop	Orange	Ylang-Ylang

2. DISPEL ANGRY CHI

Words and feelings associated with angry chi: destructive thoughts, rage, temper, frustration, irritation, frenzy, fury, outbursts

Mudra: Journey Roots into Earth

a Imagine moving angry energy as you press downward with your arms/hands, like the roots of a tree growing into the grounding, healing Mother Earth.

b Move in a slow, deliberate, relaxed way. Feel calm, knowing that all is well as you do this.

Essential Oils to Dispel Angry Chi

Angelica	Chamomile, Roman	Fir, Silver	Melissa (Lemon Balm)
Anise	Clary Sage	Frankincense	Neroli
Bay Laurel	Clementine	Galbanum	Orange
Bergamot	Coriander	Juniper	Patchouli
Blood Orange	Cypress	Lavandin	Rose, Turkish
Cardamom	Eucalyptus	Lavender	Vanilla Extract
Cedarwood	Fennel	Litsea	
Chamomile, German	Fir, Douglas	Marjoram	

3. DISPEL SAD CHI

Words and feelings associated with sad chi: heartbroken, miserable, cheerless, gloomy, disappointed

Mudra: Lotus Flower to Sun

a Start with hands in prayer position.

b Move your hands up, imagining them pushing through earth, mud, and water.

c Create the feeling of blossoming into the warmth and happiness of the sun. Look up to light!

Essential Oils to Dispel Sad Chi

Angelica	Grapefruit	Rose
Basil	Jasmine	Rose Geranium
Bergamot	Juniper	Sage
Blood Orange	Lavender	Sandalwood
Cardamom	Lemon	Spearmint
Chamomile, Roman	Neroli	Spruce
Citronella	Orange	Vetiver
Eucalyptus	Patchouli	Ylang-Ylang
Fennel	Peppermint	
Frankincense	Petitgrain	

4. Dispel Tense Chi

Words and feelings associated with tense chi: anxious, over-wrought, nervous, edgy, stressed, uptight, on edge, apprehensive, perfectionism, resentment, bitterness, pressured

Mudra: Crystal Water Flicks

a Scoop up sacred, still water in your hands and draw it toward your chest.

b Flick out through your fingertips onto the earth, releasing all tension with it.

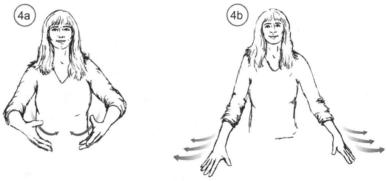

Essential Oils to Dispel Tense Chi

Bay Laurel	Juniper	Sandalwood
Bergamot	Lavandin	Spearmint
Cardamom	Lavender	Spruce
Chamomile, Roman	Marjoram	Valerian
Coriander	Melissa (Lemon Balm)	Vetiver
Cypress	Palmarosa	Ylang-Ylang
Fennel	Patchouli	
Geranium	Pine	

5. DISPEL FEARFUL CHI

Words and feelings associated with fearful chi: dread, panic, scared, lack of self-esteem, judged, trepidation, intimidated, abused, apprehension, misled, unsafe, threatened, robbed (physically or emotionally)

Mudra: Warrior Awakens

ⓐ Begin with your hands in fists, arms crossed in front of your chest in a "safety position": head down, eyes closed.

ⓑ Swiftly lift your head and open your eyes while throwing your arms out and down, palms open wide. The warrior within awakens, ready to face fears with strength and power.

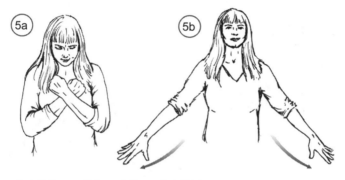

Essential Oils to Dispel Fearful Chi

Angelica	Cypress	Myrtle	Rose, Turkish
Bay Laurel	Fennel	Neroli	Rosemary
Bergamot	Fir, Douglas	Orange	Sandalwood
Cedarwood	Ginger	Oregano	Spearmint
Chamomile, Roman	Juniper	Palmarosa	Tea Tree
	Lavender	Pepper, Black	Vanilla Extract
Clary Sage	Melissa (Lemon Balm)	Rose Geranium	Vetiver
Clove			

6. DISPEL CHAOTIC CHI

Words and feelings associated with chaotic chi: disorganized, confused, muddled disarray, messy, hectic, frenzied, unruly

Mudra: Drop Blue Pearl into Calm Sea

a Start with index fingers and thumbs of both hands together in front of your chest. Imagine a glowing blue pearl held between your fingers.

b With one hand, pick up the blue pearl and move it out across your body, then drop it into the calm sea. Envision the slight ripples of the water as the pearl is dropped.

c Repeat Step B with the other hand.

(Variation: both hands take pearl out in front of body to drop it.)

Essential Oils to Dispel Chaotic Chi

Bay Laurel	Coriander	Lavandin	Rose Geranium
Bergamot	Cypress	Lavender	Rose, Turkish
Blood Orange	Eucalyptus	Lemon Verbena	Sandalwood
Cajeput	Fennel	Melissa (Lemon Balm)	Savory
Camphor	Fir, Silver		Spruce
Cardamom	Frankincense	Moroccan Mint	Tea Tree
Cedarwood	Galbanum	Neroli	Valerian
Chamomile, Roman	Hyssop	Patchouli	Vetiver
	Jasmine	Petitgrain	Ylang-Ylang
Clary Sage	Juniper	Pine, Mountain	

7. Dispel Hopeless Chi

Words and feelings associated with hopeless chi: directionless, lost, desolate, no focus, at loose ends, floundering, worry, discouraged, powerless, bleak, dreary, miserable, drab, lonely, abandoned, discouraged, invisible, insignificant, rejected, left out

Mudra: Wise Emperor Points the Way

a Hold your hands together in front of your chest, first two fingers touching, other fingers curled into fists.

b Draw one arm back and point one arm forward, turning your body to the side and pointing your index and middle fingers, like you're drawing a bow.

c Repeat the stance on the opposite side. Feel focused and strong.

Essential Oils to Dispel Hopeless Chi

Basil	Geranium	Oregano	Sage
Blood Orange	Grapefruit	Palmarosa	Sandalwood
Cedarwood	Jasmine	Patchouli	Savory
Cinnamon Leaf	Lemon	Peppermint	Spearmint
Clove	Lemon Verbena	Petitgrain	Tarragon
Cypress	Lime	Pine, Mountain	Thyme
Eucalyptus	Litsea	Ravintsara	Wintergreen
Fennel	Myrrh	Rose Geranium	Yarrow, Blue
Fir, Douglas	Neroli	Rose, Turkish	Ylang-Ylang
Frankincense	Orange	Rosemary	

8. DISPEL GUARDED CHI

Words and feelings associated with guarded chi: cynical, skeptical, suspicious, violated, untrusting, untrusted, unsafe, protecting oneself, hiding from life, lied about, lied to, misled, judged

Mudra: Soaring Bow of Ship

ⓐ Start with your hands in prayer position.

ⓑ Take a deep breath; as you release it, pull your arms back and down, sticking your chest out, like the mermaid on the bow of a ship sailing powerful and free. You are safe.

Essential Oils to Dispel Guarded Chi

Angelica Root	Clove	Myrrh	Sandalwood
Anise	Cypress	Oregano	Spearmint
Basil	Eucalyptus	Palmarosa	Spruce
Bay Laurel	Fennel	Patchouli	Tea Tree
Bergamot	Fir, Douglas	Peppermint	Thyme
Blood Orange	Frankincense	Pepper, Black	Vetiver
Cardamom	Ginger	Pine, Swiss	Wintergreen
Cedarwood	Grapefruit	Rose Geranium	Yarrow, Blue
Chamomile, Roman	Jasmine	Rosemary	
Citronella	Lemongrass	Sage	

9. DISPEL LACK OF SELF-WORTH CHI

Words and feelings associated with lack of self-worth chi: shame, embarrassment, humiliation, ridicule, guilt, not worthy, not good enough, beaten down, underestimated, disrespected, inferiority, disrespected, insignificant, unimportant, unsupported, underestimated, unloved, unlovable

Mudra: Luscious Fruit in Hand

ⓐ Start with your hands at waist level with arms out. Slowly circle your palms first, then move your arms up with wider and faster circular movements. Continue in large, fluid circular motions from the wrists; feel life's luscious, golden fruit in your hands. Fruit and seeds are self-sustaining life.

ⓑ Repeat Step A with arms at shoulder level.

ⓒ Repeat Step A with arms at head level.

Essential Oils to Dispel Lack of Self-Worth Chi

Angelica Root	Frankincense	Lime	Rosemary
Anise	Ginger	Litsea	Sandalwood
Bay Laurel	Grapefruit	Myrtle	Spruce
Bergamot	Iris	Neroli	Spearmint
Blood Orange	Jasmine	Patchouli	Sage
Cardamom	Juniper	Peppermint	Thyme
Cedarwood	Lavender	Petitgrain	Vetiver
Eucalyptus	Lemon	Rose Geranium	Ylang-Ylang
Fir, Douglas	Lemongrass	Rose, Turkish	

10. Dispel Lack Of Freedom Chi

Words and feelings associated with lack of freedom chi: contained, restricted, suffocated, trapped, imprisoned, inhibited, manipulated, controlled, obligated, people pleaser, puts others' needs first (always), pressured

Mudra: Eagle Ascending

ⓐ Spread your fingers out wide, like the tips of an eagle's wings; draw your hands up from your waist to above your head.

ⓑ Raise your arms out wide and look up, while stepping out with one foot, like an eagle ready to burst into flight.

Essential Oils to Dispel Lack of Freedom Chi

Angelica Root	Chamomile, Roman	Lemongrass	Rose Geranium
Anise		Myrtle	Rose, Turkish
Basil	Cypress	Neroli	Rosemary
Bergamot	Eucalyptus	Orange	Sage
Cardamom	Ginger	Oregano	Savory
Cajeput	Grapefruit	Palmarosa	Wintergreen
Chamomile, German	Jasmine	Pepper, Black	Ylang-Ylang
	Lemon	Pine	

ACTIVATING
Mudras

1. ACTIVATE JOY

Words and feelings associated with joy: delight, happiness, pleasure, enjoyment, bliss, euphoria, elation, jubilation, ecstasy

Mudra: Casting Petals into the Wind

ⓐ Reach down and across your body, as if pulling flowers from a basket.

ⓑ Draw the "flowers" across your chest and fling them up and out into the wind, like a carefree flower girl in a wedding on a breezy summer day.

Essential Oils to Activate Joy

Anise	Ginger	Neroli Absolute	Rose Geranium
Cardamom	Grapefruit	Orange	Rose, Turkish
Citronella	Jasmine	Pepper, Black	Savory
Clementine	Lemon	Peppermint	Vanilla Extract
Eucalyptus	Lemon Verbena	Petitgrain	Ylang-Ylang
Frankincense	Myrtle	Pine, Mountain	

2. ACTIVATE LOVE

Words and feelings associated with love: affection, adoration, friendship, kindness, tenderness, fondness, devotion, caring for, being cared for, darling, sweetheart, passion, romance

Mudra: Light of Sun Illuminates the World

a Raise your arms to sun, saying, "May the light of the sun illuminate my heart . . ."

b Draw your arms in toward your chest.

c Embrace your heart, feeling the warmth pumping through your heart and into your veins.

d Say " . . . and illuminate the world." Expand your arms out, letting the warmth flow out into the world through your fingertips.

Essential Oils to Activate Love

Ginger	Melissa (Lemon Balm)	Patchouli	Tangerine
Jasmine		Rose Absolute	Vanilla Extract
Juniper	Neroli	Rose Geranium	Ylang-Ylang
	Orange	Rose, Turkish	

3. Activate Peace

Words and feelings associated with peace: calm, quietness, stillness, tranquility, silence, harmony, balance, concord, accord, agreement

Mudra: Mountain Reflected in Still Lake

a With your right hand, touch your index finger and thumb in front of chest, like a grand mountain.

b At the same time, hold your left hand at your waist, palm facing up like the still water of a mountain lake.

Essential Oils to Activate Peace

Cedarwood	Juniper	Rose Geranium
Chamomile, Roman	Lavandin	Rose, Turkish
Clary Sage	Lavender	Rosemary
Coriander	Lemongrass	Sage
Cypress	Marjoram	Sandalwood
Elemi	Myrrh	Spearmint
Fennel	Neroli	Spruce
Fir, Silver	Oregano	Valerian
Frankincense	Patchouli	Yarrow, Blue
Galbanum	Palmarosa	Ylang-Ylang
Hyssop	Peppermint	
Jasmine	Pine, Mountain	

4. ACTIVATE VITALITY

Words and feelings associated with vitality: energy, vivacity, liveliness, drive, fervor, eagerness, strength, power, life force, vigor, gusto, zeal, zest, radiance, sparkle, spirit, dynamism, enthusiasm

Mudra: Spin Gold Light into Starlight

a Start with arms at your waist, spinning hands and arms around together in front of your body.

b Raise your arms up while continuing to spin them up above your head, then fling your hands out, throwing the golden light to connect to the stars.

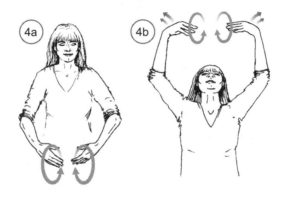

Essential Oils to Activate Vitality

Anise	Frankincense	Moroccan Mint	Rose Geranium
Basil	Ginger	Myrrh	Rose, Turkish
Cajeput	Grapefruit	Myrtle	Rosemary
Cinnamon Leaf	Jasmine	Orange	Sage
Citronella	Juniper	Peppermint	Savory
Cypress	Lemon	Petitgrain	Spearmint
Eucalyptus	Lemon Verbena	Pine, Mountain	Tea Tree
Fir, Douglas	Lime	Pine, Swiss	

5. ACTIVATE CLARITY

Words and feelings associated with clarity: focus, wisdom, intuition, clarity, lucidity, precision, centered, direct, lack of confusion, straightforward

Mudra: Diamond in the Sky

ⓐ Create a diamond shape between your index fingers and thumbs of both hands above your head, and peer into the heavens through this diamond.

ⓑ Bring the diamond down to your forehead, then touch your fingertips to your third eye. Focus.

ⓒ Throw your arms out wide and hands back. Raise your head and imagine looking to the diamond-like stars in the sky, feeling clear and centered.

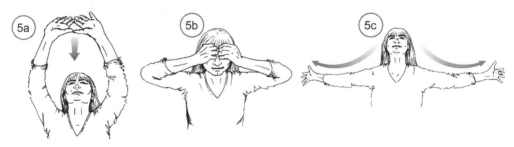

Essential Oils to Activate Clarity

Basil	Galbanum	Neroli	Spearmint
Cajeput	Hyssop	Patchouli	Tea Tree
Camphor	Juniper	Peppermint	Wintergreen
Elemi	Lemongrass	Petitgrain	Yarrow, Blue
Eucalyptus	Litsea	Pine, Mountain	Ylang-Ylang
Fir, Silver	Moroccan Mint	Rosemary	
Frankincense	Myrrh	Sage	

6. ACTIVATE COURAGE

Words and feelings associated with courage: bravery, guts, valor, nerve, gallantry, heroism, daring, pluck, willingness to take risks

Mudra: Sherpa Reaches Summit

a Reach strongly with your right hand to the clouds that graciously embrace the mountaintop; hold your left hand to your heart.

b Soften and relax your right arm, feeling the humility in the face of the grandeur of the mountain.

Essential Oils to Activate Courage

Bergamot	Cypress	Lemon Verbena	Pine
Cajeput	Eucalyptus	Lime	Ravintsara
Cedarwood	Fir, Douglas	Neroli	Sage
Cinnamon Leaf	Ginger	Oregano	Savory
Citronella	Jasmine	Patchouli	Thyme
Clove	Lemon	Pepper, Black	

7. ACTIVATE ACCEPTANCE

Words and feelings associated with acceptance: openness, sincerity, open heart, tolerant, embracing, accommodating, cherishing

Mudra: Embrace the World (and Yourself)

ⓐ Begin with your index fingers and thumbs together, arms crossed in front of your chest, head up, loving and accepting yourself.

ⓑ Draw your arms out wide, index fingers and thumbs still together, and embrace and accept the world.

ⓒ Draw your arms back in toward your chest to where you began.

Essential Oils to Activate Acceptance

Angelica Root	Fennel	Lemon Verbena	Sandalwood
Anise	Fir, Douglas	Melissa (Lemon Balm)	Spearmint
Bay Laurel	Frankincense		Vetiver
Chamomile, German	Galbanum	Neroli	Yarrow, Blue
	Iris	Patchouli	Ylang-Ylang
Chamomile, Roman	Juniper	Rose Geranium	
Cypress	Lavender	Rose, Turkish	

8. Activate Strength

Words and feelings associated with a sense of strength: power, endurance, authority, command, inner control, determination, fortitude, stamina, staying power, resilience

Mudra: Ancient Rock Withstands the Sea

ⓐ Stand strong with feet apart, knees slightly bent, hands in fists, and arms held in front of your body like a boxer.

ⓑ Imagine you are an ancient rock, able to withstand pounding waves and weather for centuries. Solid. Everlasting.

Essential Oils to Activate Strength

Basil	Ginger	Pine, Swiss	Savory
Cajeput	Neroli	Ravintsara	Thyme
Cedarwood	Pepper, Black	Sage	
Fir, Douglas	Pine		

STEPS
OF
Elemental
SPACE CLEARING

The steps of Elemental Space Clearing do not vary wildly from those you learned in Chapter 2, which outlines the four stages of space clearing. However, you'll also do specific mudras at different steps. Dispelling and and activating mudras, which we covered in the previous sections, are used during the space clearing as needed. Initiation mudras are done at the beginning of your clearing. You will find the diagrams for the initiation mudras listed in this guide on pages 193 to 196, numbered 1 through 28. In the following pages, each step with a relevant diagram has the diagram number noted in parentheses with the letter *d* (e.g., d1).

—— STAGE 1: PREPARATION ——

A. Prepare Tools

1. Set Up Blessing Altar

- Choose altar cloth
- Choose and cleanse items, such as crystals or small figurines, for your altar
- Prepare Blessing Tray (optional)

2. Choose Tools for Breaking Up Energy (Bells, etc.)

- Cleanse the tools
- Attune the tools

3. Choose Tools for Smoothing Energy (Feather, Chimes, etc.)

- Cleanse the tools
- Attune the tools

4. Choose Oils

- Intuitively choose oils to use for each stage: preparation oil(s), purification oil(s), invocation oil(s), and preservation oil(s). (See pages 155 through 157.)

B. Prepare Yourself Before Clearing

1. Meditation

- Call upon your guides
- Communicate with the oversoul spirit of the plant/flower of your chosen essential oils for the four stages

2. Breath Techniques

- Take deep breaths
- Inhale the scent of the essential oil or oils that you chose for the preparation stage (to activate inner qualities within you for space clearing)

3. Nature

- Spend time in nature or visualizing and absorbing energy of the elements

4. Choose Clothes for Space Clearing

- Make sure that the clothes that you choose are clean
- Pick colors and textures that are in alignment with your clearing

C. Prepare Yourself Immediately Before Space Clearing

1. Meditate

- Take time to meditate on and visualize the task before you. Visualize the space shimmering and becoming bright with energy.

2. Drink Lots of Water

3. Cleanse Yourself

4. Remove Jewelry, Particularly Rings and Bracelets

D. Activating Your Intention

1. Finding True Intention for Space Clearing

- What is your intention for yourself?
- What is your intention for the space?

2. Refining Focus for Intention

- "See" the positive outcome: now and in the future
- "Affirm" the outcome: deepen focus
- Use your "preparation oil(s)" along with the initiation mudra that assists your "Manifestation of Intention." (See d1a, d1b, d2, and d3 on page 193.) Rub/Open Arms/Into Heart/Snap and Out.

E. *Place Your Tools and Objects on the Altar*

1. Unfold Your Altar Cloth

2. Prepare Your Tools (see d4 and d5 for examples of altar setups)

3. Place Candle (Flowers Optional)

4. Light Oil Burner and Add Drops of Purification Oil(s) (Optional)

5. Pray for Guidance and Support

—— STAGE 2: PURIFICATION ——

A. *At Altar, Put Three Drops of "Purification Oil(s)" into Hands*

1. Each Drop Is in Honor of the Divinity of Self, All Beings, and the Creator

- Do this slowly and deliberately, feeling the prayer with each drop

2. Rub Hands Together

- Connect with the oversoul of the specific plant(s) in your chosen essential oils for the purification stage

3. Hands in Prayer Position

- Hold intention for specific purification

4. Place Hands in Front of Face (d6) and Inhale Three Times: In Dedication to Self, All Beings, and the Creator

5. Gently Use Hands to Infuse Tools (Stones, Bell, Feather, etc.) with Essence of Plant/Flower Energy

- Put hands in prayer position (d7), then open palms to make a gateway for heart energy to flow through (d8)

- Project energy through palms to tools (d9)

- Say a prayer, aloud or silently, and call for spiritual assistance and support

B. Igniting the Sacred Point between Heaven and Earth: To Balance Your Energy at the Beginning of the Space Clearing

1. Stand at Entrance to Room

2. Hands in Prayer Position: Holding Intention in Heart (d10)

3. To Balance Your Energy and Align Your Chakras, Use Mudra "You Are the Center Point for Heaven and Earth"

- Rotate right hand on top of left (d11) (yang over yin/ Heaven over Earth) with downward motion toward first chakra (d12). Say and feel: "I am the center point between Heaven and Earth."

- Bring hands up to heart chakra and rotate into prayer position (d13)

- Bring hands in prayer position to third eye (touch third eye with thumbs with fingers pointing skyward) (d14)

- Bring hands back to prayer position (d15)

- Rotate left hand on top of right hand (d16) (earth/yin over heaven/yang) with downward motion towards first chakra. Say and feel: "I am the center point between Earth and Heaven."

- Bring hands up to heart chakra and then to third eye. Repeat this movement two more times while doing the mudras. Say and feel: "I am the center point between Earth and Heaven."

C. Igniting the Sacred Point Between Heaven and Earth: To Balance Your Home's Energy at the Beginning of the Space Clearing

1. Use Mudra "This Home Is the Center of Heaven and Earth." Do these motions in a slow and deliberate manner with serene intent. Repeat the entire mudra nine times.

- Hold hands in prayer position (d17)

- Arms up over your head (d18), inhale

- Palms turn outward (d19)
- Call the heavens into the home as palms and arms come down
- Slowly (d20) exhale as arms come down
- Arms extend downward with fingers almost touching (d21)
- Palms up—calling the earth upward—bring arms up to chest (d22)
- Inhale as arms move up and then pivot into prayer position (d23)
- Exhale while in prayer position

D. Use Tools, Elemental Mudras, and Oils

1. Circle Each Room with Your Tools (If Using)

- Feel and dispel or activate the energy in the room as needed. You can use any of the mudras described in this chapter, alone or with tools.

2. Complete Each Room with a Figure-Eight and Blessing (Aloud or Silently)

- This seals in the wonderful energy that you have called into the space, so that every person who enters the room is uplifted.

——— Stage 3: Dedication ———
(Invocation and Blessing)

A. Return to Altar

1. Light Candle and Say Blessing Prayer

2. Use Your "Invocation Oil(s)"

- Place three drops in hand for self, others, Creator

- Rub and hold intent of dedication (with hands in prayer position)

3. Focus on Candle or (Optional) Light Fire/Charcoal for Blessing Resins

- Dip hands into smoke (d24) (or above the candle flame) . . . up to heart (d25), then out to home (d26). Repeat nine times.

- Say, "May this home be filled with . . . "

4. Call Spirit/Ancestors/Spirit Guides/Angels

- Hold hands in prayer position while calling (d27)

5. Give Thanks for the Blessings Received

- Hold palms up (d28)

6. Put Items Away with Grace and Ease

- Cleanse tools and self afterward

B. After Clearing

1. When you have completed the clearing, bless the home and the occupants

2. Leave flower offering with incense or scented candles in each room (optional)

3. Cleanse and bless each household member (optional)

4. Finish with the completion blessing ceremony at the altar

5. Wash hands with cool water all the way to the elbows. Shake your hands a few times before you dry them.

——— STAGE 4: PRESERVATION ———
(GROUNDING, PROTECTING, AND SUSTAINING)

Once you have purified a space and blessed it, do the following to preserve the wonderful energy that you have created:

- *Bathing:* It is valuable for everyone, including you and other members of the household, to bathe within six hours after an extensive space clearing. Doing this not only cleanses the body but also symbolically refreshes the spirit and helps preserve the energy you have created in your home. A simple bath or shower with a cold rinse is fine, but bathing in salt water is especially beneficial.

    Salt bath: Dissolve ½ pound (8 oz.) of regular salt or Epsom salt in the bathwater.

    Salt shower: Rub your body with salt before showering, ending with a cold rinse.

There are a few other methods from which you can choose to further sustain the energy:

- *Planting a prayer:* Write a prayer or blessing on a piece of paper during your completion at the Blessing Altar and bury it in a favorite plant in the home. Every time the plant is watered, the prayer will be symbolically energized.

- *Symbols:* Draw a symbol or write a special word on a stone, then tuck it away by the front door, by a plant, or in an elevated place in the home.

- *Stones:* Leave a stone (or several stones) in a special place in the house to radiate energy. (See Appendix B for guidance on choosing stones.)

- *Oil blend:* If you chose "preservation oil(s)" for the clearing, you can put it into a small mister, burner, or diffuser.

- *An object from the Blessing Altar:* Place an object from the Blessing Altar such as a figurine of an angel, crystal, or some other representation of the divine realms in a special place in the home.

INITIATION

Mudras

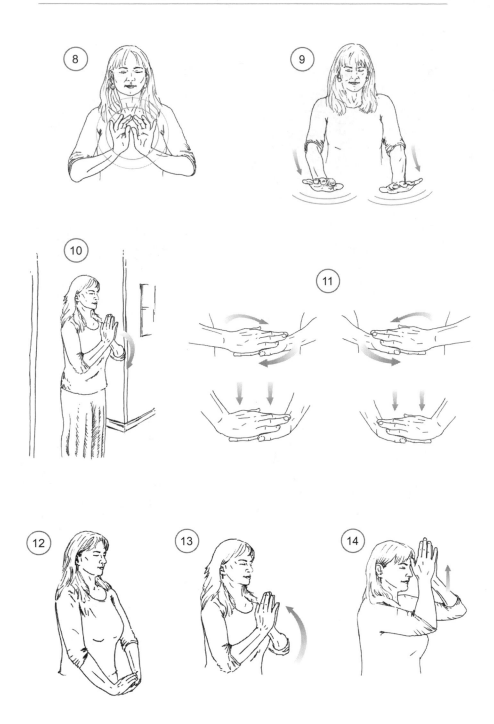

Harmony *in the* Home, Your Life, *and* Our World

All life is energy. Physicists acknowledge that underlying the energy of atoms and molecules is a constant motion. They declare what ancient mystics have always known: beneath the surface of physical objects, energy swirls into form, dissolves, and coalesces once again. The world is in a constant dance of fluid patterns of ebbing and flowing energy. Underlying this motion is a cosmic order, an innate harmony in all life. However, as huge changes in technology have occurred, we have lost this fundamental balance.

The ancient wisdom of space clearing is an organic and natural way to reclaim balance and harmony in our homes and in our lives. As you step into this sacred tradition, you understand that every object in your home affects your energy in a different way. The more you open up your heart and inner awareness to the realm of energy, the more you will hear the voice of everything in your surroundings. As you refine your ability to sense energy, you will notice when your home is out of balance, and you will intuitively know what is needed to restore harmony. This is an intuitive art. Like any art, the more you practice, the more refined your skills will become.

There is great power in small sacred acts. When you listen to your own inner wisdom, you will know what you need to do. When you space clear your home and call forth blessings for the people who live there, it is a sacred act. You generate a beautiful energy field that travels in ripples beyond the boundaries of your home into the universe around you, bringing a sense of grace, beauty, and love to all in ways that you may never be aware.

When you clear and bless your home or business, this generates an extraordinary energy that radiates in all directions, positively influencing the surrounding area. Human beings are one small part of something grand and infinite, and even more wonderful than we can ever imagine. Though we are not often aware of it, when we open our hearts to the promptings of Spirit, this creates an energy that has an enormous impact on the universe around us. People you don't know and may never know will be influenced by what you do. Whenever you space clear, you are making a difference in the world.

As you begin to understand the profound nature of space clearing, you will tap into an immense current of love, harmony, and power that helps us be part of something much bigger than our individual identities. Space clearing can help you connect with a divine force that can offer protection, purification, and blessings for your home and, ultimately, for the world. And with each space you clear, each blessing you create, the ripples of your work will spread throughout the world.

RECOMMENDED
Resources

If you find yourself becoming more passionate about energy and environments, you might be interested in taking my courses to learn even more ways to work with the energy of a space:

To become certified as a professional space clearer, consider taking my online course in Elemental Space Clearing®: www.elementalspaceclearing.com.

Interior Alignment® is a feng shui and space clearing system I created that uses ancient wisdom from cultures all over the world. In this system, you not only can expand your knowledge of space clearing practices, but you can also learn the art of feng shui and powerful ways to work with clients, using my Synchro-Alignment Process. You will learn about clutter clearing, the Seven Star Blessing Space Clearing™, and environmentally healthy home issues, so that each living space you clear can be as uplifting and healthy as possible. The Interior Alignment® program provides valuable information on how to structure your space clearing and feng shui business. For more information about Interior Alignment, its curriculum, and upcoming certification programs, please visit www.InteriorAlignment.com.

If you'd like to find a certified practitioner in your area or become a certified professional, please visit: The Linn Academy: http://thelinnacademy.com.

APPENDIX A

Reference Guide *to* Colors

Color impacts us physically, emotionally, and spiritually. Our response to light is deeply ingrained in our nervous system. The enzymes and hormones in our bodies are affected by different colored lights, causing them to go through molecular changes.

Our spectrum of consciousness is not separate from the spectrum of light. Color is a part of the radiation from the sun. Within the visible electromagnetic spectrum, the longest wavelength (lowest frequency) is red light and the shortest wavelength (highest frequency) is violet light. (White light does not have a specific frequency or wavelength because it is just what our eyes see when all the of colors' frequencies are combined.)

Because consciousness is so closely related to the spectrum of light, the colors you choose for your clothing, altar cloth, objects on your Blessing Altar, and other tools will dramatically affect the energy of your space clearing.

Refer to the following list for your altar cloths, items for your altar, and the clothes that you wear during your clearings.

red: Associated with strength, courage, steadfastness, health, vigor, passion, sensuality, fire, zest, drive, and physical energy. Revitalizing and stimulating, red can assist in overcoming inertia, depression, fear, or melancholy. It's dynamic and tenacious.

orange: Associated with optimism, expansiveness, emotional balance, confidence, self-motivation, changeability, enthusiasm, and a sense of connection and community.

yellow: Associated with clarity of thought, mental discrimination, organization, attention to detail, evaluation, active intelligence, academic achievement, discipline, administration, heightened expression, joy, and freedom. Stimulates the intellect and aids in communication.

green: Stimulates feelings of balance, harmony, peace, hope, growth, and healing. Green is found everywhere in nature, symbolizing the abundant, replenishing forces of the universe.

blue: Stimulates inspiration, creativity, spiritual understanding, faith, and devotion. Allows for gentleness, contentment, patience, and composure.

purple: Activates spiritual awareness and intuition. Stimulates our inner wisdom and connection to unseen realms. Associated with heightening spiritual perspective and intuition. Calming, soothing, and comforting.

white: Associated with purity, clarity, and transformation. White encompasses all colors and thus is the fastest wavelength of the color spectrum. It relates to divine realization, humility, and creative imagination.

black: Associated with vision, introspection, germinating, silence, incubation, and stillness.

pink: Associated with love, softness, grace, kindness, and self-nurturing.

APPENDIX B

Reference Guide
to Crystals *and* Stones
for Your Space Clearing Altar

Each type of stone or gem elicits a particular kind of energy. Some activate healing, some soothe and relax, and others evoke vitality.

agate: success, happiness

amber: protection, healing

amethyst: compassion, clairvoyance

aquamarine: harmony

aventurine: healing

bloodstone: healing, physical strengthening

carnelian: physical grounding

citrine: mental clarity

emerald: spiritual healing

fluorite: mental attunement, calming

garnet: physical strength, assertiveness

jade: healing, wisdom

lapis: spirituality, intuition, royalty

malachite: psychic power, healing, cleansing

moonstone: emotional balancing, lunar qualities

obsidian: grounding

opal: emotional clarity

peridot: mental and physical healing, rejuvenation

prehnite: calmness, unconditional love, healing

quartz crystal: spiritual
attunement

ruby: strength, health,
spiritual passion

sapphire: devotion,
spirituality

selenite: dreaming skills,
intuition, meditation

topaz: expansion,
knowledge

tourmaline: purification,
healing

turquoise: healing,
balancing

APPENDIX C

Reference Guide
to Flowers
and Flower Essences

FLOWERS

Flowers are a wonderful way of generating energy for your space clearing. Here are a few varieties you can use and their associated qualities:

chrysanthemum: introspection, meditation, longevity

daffodil: childlike joy, laughter

daisy: innocence, happiness

iris: delicate sensuality

lily: purity, perfection

lily of the valley: springtime, new life

marigold: joy, longevity

rose: love

sunflower: optimism, joy

tulip: vitality, sensual love

violet: tenderness, trust

FLOWER ESSENCES

The following is a partial list of essences and their qualities to help get you started:

angelica: open to guidance from divine realm

angel's trumpet: deeply soothing and peaceful, spiritual initiation

Bach's Rescue Remedy blend: balances energy after trauma, argument, or illness

blackberry: manifesting, directing action, decisiveness

black-eyed Susan: awakening consciousness

cayenne: breaking free of the old, catalyst for change

centaury: brings quietness, wisdom

cerato: brings confidence, helps with decisions

chamomile: calming, soothing, good for a home that feels downtrodden

cherry plum: calming, quiet energy

clematis: dispels lethargy, ignites focus

fireweed: the best essence for releasing old patterns and attracting new, restorative energy

garlic: psychic protection for the home

gorse: positive faith in overcoming difficulties

Indian paintbrush: stimulates creativity

iris: spiritual integration

lavender: soothes tension and stress

lotus: opening spiritual consciousness that has been restricted

mimulus: minimizes fear and dread

morning glory: reawakening vigor and new life

pennyroyal: dispels negative influences

peppermint: alertness, vitality

rosemary: releases mental fog

sagebrush: releasing old habits that are no longer appropriate

Shasta daisy: focus, synthesis of ideas

star of Bethlehem: clears residues of tension from past experience

water violet: gentleness, tranquility, poise, grace

wild rose: vitality, lively interest in all things

yarrow: strengthening, excellent for protection

APPENDIX D

Reference Guide
to Essential Oils

Here are common uses and qualities for some essential oils for your space clearing. This is a partial list of only some of the many oils that can be used for space clearing. However, remember that within your soul is an innate wisdom that absolutely knows what oils are needed for a particular space. So take time to tune in to your inner knowing before you choose your oils. (With thanks to the kind folks at Primavera Essential Oils in Bavaria for some of this information.)

Allspice: Warming, expanding.

Angelica Root: Soothing, calming, invoking the angels. Assists in the release of pent-up negative feelings and restores memories to the point of origin before trauma or anger was experienced.

Anise: Opens emotional blocks and recharges vital energy.

Basil: Fights mental fatigue, stimulates, sharpens focus and attention to detail.

Bay Laurel: Calming, hormonal support, antidepressant. Relieves anxiety; mood-lifting qualities. (Do not use if pregnant.)

Bergamot: Encouraging, emotional balance, uplifting.

Birch: Cleansing, stimulating, activating.

Blood Orange: Relieves anxiety, nervousness, tension, nervous conditions.

Cajeput: Clarifying; enhances concentration, brings strength and purification.

Camphor: Refreshing, purifying, ideal for concentration.

Cardamom: Uplifting, refreshing, invigorating.

Cedarwood: Balancing, stabilizing, strengthening, gives courage, self-confidence. Stimulates the limbic system (controls emotions), stimulates pineal gland (releases melatonin). Has been shown to treat ADHD in clinical studies. Recognized for its calming, purifying properties.

Chamomile (German): Dispels anger, stabilizes emotions, and helps release emotions linked to the past. Soothes and clears the mind.

Chamomile (Roman): Because it is calming and relaxing, it can combat depression, insomnia, and stress. It minimizes anxiety, irritability, and nervousness. It may also dispel anger, stabilize the emotions, and help to release emotions that are linked to the past.

Cinnamon Bark: Warming, stimulating, joy-inducing.

Cinnamon Leaf: Enhances and promotes inspiration and creativity.

Citronella: Powerful cleansing of stagnant energies; refreshing and uplifting.

Clary Sage: Enhances one's ability to dream; calming, stress-relieving, revitalizing, relaxing, inspiring.

Clementine: Cheering, refreshing, invigorating.

Clove: Sterilizes energies, cleanses emotional wounds, mentally stimulating; encourages sleep, stimulates dreams, and creates a sense of protection and courage.

Coriander: Soothing and calming.

Cypress: Eases the feeling of loss and creates a sense of security and grounding. Helps heal emotional trauma; calms, soothes anger, and helps life flow better. Assists in concentration and structure; gathers energy.

Elemi: Its spicy incense-like fragrance is conducive to meditation. Can be grounding. Used to clear the mind.

Eucalyptus Globulus: Promotes health, well-being, purification, and healing.

Fennel: Helps relaxation; enhances balance and stability. Earthy, grounding, calms anger.

Fir, Douglas: Strengthening, good at expelling mood swings, uplifting, and concentrating.

Fir, Silver: Grounding, stimulating to the mind, and relaxing to the body.

Frankincense: Increases spiritual awareness, promotes meditation, improves attitude, uplifts spirits, elevates; grounding, protecting. Contains sesquiterpenes, which stimulate the limbic system (memory and emotion), the hypothalamus (master gland, which produces vital hormones including thyroid and growth hormones), and the pineal and pituitary glands.

Galbanum: Harmonic and balancing, amplifies spiritual awareness and meditation. (When combined with frankincense or sandalwood, the frequency rises dramatically.)

Geranium: Release depressive energy, calms.

Ginger: Gentle, stimulating, endowing physical energy, warmth, and courage.

Grapefruit: Refreshing, invigorating, and uplifting. A 1995 study found that citrus fragrances boosted immunity, induced relaxation, and reduced depression.

Hyssop: Stimulates creativity; aids in meditation.

Jasmine: Uplifting; counteracts hopelessness, nervous exhaustion, anxiety, depression, indifference, and listlessness. Has been documented to improve concentration and mental acuity.

Juniper: Evokes feelings of health, love, and peace and may help to elevate one's spiritual awareness.

Juniper Berry: Detoxifying, cleansing, uplifting.

Lavandin: Similar calming effects as lavender.

Lavender (Fine): Calming, relaxing, refreshing, and balancing, both physically and emotionally. University of Miami researchers found that inhalation of lavender oil increased beta waves in the brain, suggesting heightened relaxation. It also reduced depression and improved cognitive performance.

Lemon: Promotes clarity of thought and purpose. Astringent, toning, purifying.

Lemongrass: Promotes psychic awareness and purification. Powerful, toning, stimulating.

Lemon Verbena: Stimulating, refreshing, inspiring, motivating.

Lime: Mentally clearing and refreshing; stimulates energy and concentration; helpful for listless and tired people.

Litsea Cubeba: Refreshing, mentally clearing, lifts mood. Aroma: lemony.

Mandarin: Ignites joy, stimulates communication.

Marjoram: Assists in calming the nerves, good to overcome grief; warming.

Melissa (lemon balm): Brings out gentle characteristics within people. Calming, protecting, strengthening.

Moroccan Mint: Refreshing; increasing concentration and memory.

Myrrh: Promotes spiritual awareness and emotional balance; uplifting. Contains sesquiterpenes, which stimulate the limbic system (memory and emotion), the hypothalamus (master gland, which produces vital hormones including thyroid and growth hormones), and the pineal and pituitary glands.

Neroli: Balances mind-body-spirit.

Neroli Absolute (Egyptian, Moroccan): A natural relaxant used to treat depression and anxiety. It strengthens and stabilizes the emotions and uplifts and inspires the hopeless, encouraging confidence, courage, joy, peace, and sensuality. It brings everything into focus at the moment.

Nutmeg: Stimulates flow and circulation.

Orange: Uplifting, peace, happiness. A 1995 study found that citrus fragrances boosted immunity, induced relaxation, and reduced depression.

Oregano: Creates a feeling of security.

Palmarosa: Awakening, clarity. Creates a feeling of security. It also helps to reduce stress and tension and promotes recovery from nervous exhaustion.

Patchouli: Sensuous, grounding. A relaxant that clarifies thoughts, allowing the discarding of jealousies, obsessions, and insecurities.

Pepper, Black: Powerful stimulant, shifts stagnant energies. Warming, empowering, invigorating, aphrodisiac.

Peppermint. Refreshing, healing, invigorating; clarity. Purifying and stimulating to the conscious mind.

Peru Myrtle: Elevating and euphoric.

Petitgrain: Calming; softens rigidity. Uplifting and refreshing to the senses; it clears confusion, reduces mental fatigue and depression. Stimulates the mind and improves memory.

Pine: Regenerates, purifies; new beginnings.

Pine (Mountain): Stimulating, concentrating, purifying, energizing, and strengthening.

Pine (Needle): Relieves anxiety and revitalizes mind, body, and spirit.

Pine (Swiss): Strengthening, cleansing, regenerative.

Ravintsara: Purifying, strengthening, and refreshing.

Rose (Alba, Attar, Bourbon, Bulgarian): Helps bring balance and harmony, allowing one to overcome insecurities. It is stimulating and elevating to the mind, creating a sense of well-being.

Rose (Turkish): Brings balance and harmony, allowing one to overcome insecurities. Stimulating and elevating to the mind, creates a sense of well-being.

Rose Geranium: Helps release negative memories and eases nervous tension. It balances the emotions, lifts the spirit, and fosters peace, well-being, and hope.

Rosemary: Clarity; stimulating, strengthening. Helps overcome mental fatigue and improves mental clarity and focus.

Rosewood: Warming, woody, earthy.

Sage: Ceremonial cleansing, purifying. Mentally stimulating and helps combat despair and mental fatigue. Sage strengthens the vital centers of the body, balancing the pelvic chakra where negative emotions from denial and abuse are stored.

Sandalwood: Harmonizing, opening to spirit, slowing. Enhances deep sleep; may help remove negative programming from the cells. It is high in sesquiterpenes, which stimulate the pineal gland (responsible for releasing melatonin, a powerful immune stimulant and antitumoral agent) and the limbic region of the brain, the center of emotions. Can be grounding and stabilizing.

Spearmint: Opens and releases emotional blocks and brings about a feeling of balance and lasting sense of well-being. Uplifting, invigorating, rejuvenating.

Spruce: Opens and helps release emotional blockages, bringing about a feeling of balance and grounding.

Tangerine: Calming, soothing, happiness.

Tea Tree: Promotes cleansing and purity.

Thyme: Antiseptic, cleansing. May be beneficial in helping to overcome fatigue and exhaustion after illness.

Valerian: Deep relaxation, grounding.

Vetiver: Psychologically grounding, calming, and stabilizing. It helps us to cope with stress and recover from emotional trauma.

Vetiver: Stress release; grounding, regenerating.

Wintergreen: Stimulates and increases awareness in all levels of the sensory system.

Yarrow, Blue: Balancing highs and lows, both external and internal, yarrow simultaneously inspires and grounds us. Useful during meditation and supportive to intuitive energies. Reduces confusion and ambivalence.

Ylang-Ylang: Balances male-female energies, enhances spiritual attunement, combats anger, combats low self-esteem, and increases focus of thoughts; filters out negative energy. Restores confidence, peace, and balance. Ignites romantic love.

AROMAS AND BLEND SUGGESTIONS

To inspire you to create your own blends, here is additional information about which scents combine well with others and for what purpose. Though, as always, follow your nose and your own intuition.

Basil: *Aroma:* herbal, sweet, fresh, green. *Blends well with* lemon, lemongrass, orange, rose.

Bergamot: *Aroma:* fruity, green, lively. *Blends well with* neroli, rose, vetiver, lavender, citrus oils, ylang-ylang.

Blood Orange: *Aroma:* fruity, fresh, sweet. *Blends well with* vanilla, peppermint, citrus oils.

Cajeput: *Aroma:* eucalyptus-like

Cardamom: *Aroma:* aromatic, green, woody-balsamic.

Cedarwood: *Aroma:* balsamic, soft, woody, herbal, sweet, warm. *Blends well with* rose, bergamot, lavender, jasmine, neroli, juniper, orange.

Chamomile (German): *Aroma:* intense, herbal, sweet.

Chamomile (Roman): *Aroma:* delicate, floral, fruity, sweet, clean. *Blends well with* rose, lavender, cedar, lemongrass, neroli, rose geranium, bergamot.

Clary Sage: *Aroma:* warm, herbal, sweet, light, hay-like. *Blends well with* jasmine, sandalwood, geranium, cypress, lavender, orange, bergamot, rosemary, sandalwood, ylang-ylang.

Cypress: *Aroma:* dry, resinous, smoky, warm, spicy, ambergris. *Blends well with* bergamot, clary sage, lemon, lavender, orange, lime, juniper, pine.

Eucalyptus Dives: *Aroma:* fresh, invigorating.

Eucalyptus Globulus: *Aroma:* fresh, clean, stimulating. *Blends well with* lemon, peppermint, thyme.

Fennel: *Aroma:* warm, sweet, aniseed-like. *Blends well with* lavender, rose geranium, Melissa (lemon balm).

Fir, Douglas: *Aroma:* clear, fresh, citrus-like.

Fir, Silver: *Aroma:* fresh, clear, woody, green.
Blends well with neroli, citrus oils.

Frankincense: *Aroma:* warm, woody, sweet.
Blends well with rose, cedarwood.

Ginger:
Aroma: fiery hot, spicy.

Hyssop: *Aroma:* aromatic, spicy, fresh.
Blends well with lavender, sage, rosemary, lemon verbena, clary sage.

Jasmine:
Aroma: feminine, sensual, intense, honey sweet.
Blends well with rose, neroli, sandalwood, orange, cypress, cedarwood.

Lavender (Fine): *Aroma:* fresh, floral, clear, pure.
Blends well with clary sage, cedarwood, rosemary, tea tree.

Lemon Verbena: *Aroma:* elegant, lemony.
Blends well with neroli, jasmine, orange, juniper, hyssop, myrtle, cedarwood.

Lemon:
Aroma: fresh, clean, sunny.
Blends well with thyme, eucalyptus, citrus, lavender, pine, cedar, fennel, juniper.

Lemongrass:
Aroma: fresh, cool, clean, strong, highly radiant, citrus.
Blends well with pine, eucalyptus, juniper, rose geranium, lavender, citrus oils.

Litsea Cubeba:
Aroma: lemony.

Melissa (lemon balm):
Aroma: smooth, warm, fresh.
Blends well with lavender, rose, chamomile (Roman).

Moroccan Mint:
Aroma: refreshing.
Blends well with eucalyptus, lavender, rosemary, grapefruit; mint fragrance dominates.

Neroli: *Aroma:* delicate, fresh, floral, sweet.
Blends well with vanilla, citrus oils.

Neroli Absolute (Egyptian, Moroccan): *Aroma:* spicy, highly radiant.
Blends well with rose, lavender, sandalwood, jasmine, cedar, geranium, lemon.

Orange:
Aroma: fruity, sweet, warm.
Blends well with cedarwood,

Melissa (lemon balm), rose, fennel, citrus oils, coriander, cinnamon, ylang-ylang, sandalwood, neroli, juniper, cypress.

Patchouli:
Aroma: earthy, exotic, warm.
Blends well with rose, citrus oils.

Pepper, Black:
Aroma: intense, spicy.

Peppermint:
Aroma: fresh, cool, clean.
Blends well with grapefruit, rosemary.

Peru Myrtle:
Aroma: fresh, herbal, similar to sage and eucalyptus.
Blends well with pine, lemon, neroli, cypress, lavender.

Petitgrain: *Aroma:* fresh, flowery, revitalizing, slightly resembling neroli.

Pine (Mountain): *Aroma:* fresh, clear, woody-resinous.

Pine (Needle): *Aroma:* empowering yet grounding.

Pine (Swiss): *Aroma:* strengthening, cleansing, regenerative.
Blends well with eucalyptus, lemon, lemon verbena, juniper, lemongrass, grapefruit, angelica, myrtle, cajeput, birch.

Ravintsara:
Aroma: clear and pungent.

Rose (Alba, Attar, Bourbon, Bulgarian):
Aroma: stimulating and elevating.
Blends well with neroli, lavender, sandalwood, jasmine.

Rose (Turkish):
Aroma: full, heavy, floral.
Blends well with sandalwood, lavender, Melissa (lemon balm), vanilla, orange, jasmine.

Rose Geranium:
Aroma: warm, sunny floral.
Blends well with grapefruit, cedarwood.

Rosemary:
Aroma: clear, fresh, spicy.
Blends well with citrus oils, fir, peppermint, tea tree.

Sandalwood:
Aroma: warm, balsam-like, sweet, woody, velvety, exotic.
Blends well with rose, ylang-ylang, benzoin, jasmine, lemon verbena, frankincense, cedarwood, patchouli, vetiver.

Silver Fir: *Aroma:* fresh, clear, woody, green.
Blends well with neroli, citrus oils.

Tea Tree: *Aroma:* spicy, herbal, pungent, fresh.

Blends well with lavender, chamomile.

Thyme:
Aroma: herbal, fresh, spicy.
Blends well with citrus oils.

Vanilla Extract:
Aroma: sweet, warm.
Blends well with rose, orange.

Vetiver: *Aroma:* earthy, heavy, musty, woody, dark. *Blends well with* orange, sandalwood, lemon verbena, geranium, ylang-ylang, jasmine, cedarwood.

Yarrow, Blue:
Aroma: herbal, resinous, warm, aromatic.
Blends well with lemongrass, hyssop, clary sage, myrtle.

Ylang-Ylang:
Aroma: feminine, exotic, sweet, soft, flowery, erotic.
Blends well with sandalwood, orange, jasmine, neroli, rose, cedarwood.

APPENDIX E

Reference Guide *to* Ghosts

Some people have certain experiences or feelings about a space that cause them to believe there is a ghost in their dwelling. Sometimes there is an actual ghost, in which case they may need to employ a professional to help release it. But almost always what is perceived as a ghost is actually predecessor energy or residual energy, which can be cleared by space clearing. In this Appendix, we'll discuss what ghosts are and what common energies you may be mistaking for a ghost.

GHOSTS

Ghosts are beings who have become stuck between this plane of existence and the next, caught in a kind of limbo. For the most part, the ghost doesn't know that it's dead; this is sometimes because of a traumatic passing. They may be attached to the earth plane because of a strong bond to a person or an addiction. Addictive cravings—such as those to food, drugs, or alcohol—can be so strong that the ghost has trouble leaving the earth plane.

There are three indicators that let you know you are seeing a ghost:

- Usually appears again and again and is seen by a number of people
- Can be "seen" as a mist or a more solid shape
- Associated with a particular place

How You Might Sense a Ghost

Some people have a fuller spectrum of "seeing" that allows them to see auras, elementals, and ghosts. However, for the most part, when we talk about a ghost that is "seen" or "heard," it doesn't mean through our physical eyes or ears.

First, remember that our perception of the world around us occurs because our senses—eyes, ears, nose, etc.—gather information and then relay it to our brain. This information is screened and enhanced by the mind according to our beliefs and our need for survival. The way we "see" the world—our perception—resides not in the senses but in the brain. For example, hallucinations are superimposed images, sounds, smells, and so forth that are added to (or alternatively, blocked or deleted from) the data received by the senses.

In the same way, the energy field of a ghost somehow contributes information to the other data received by the senses. This is then all integrated into what our brain perceives. In other words, the energy field of ghosts provides our brains with extra information necessary to "see" them.

If you have any of the following experiences without any physical source or underlying cause, it may indicate the presence of a ghost:

- sudden coolness
- dampness
- heavy feeling
- difficulty breathing
- depression
- lights going on and off
- doors opening and closing
- the feeling of a light touch
- just a "feeling" (most common)
- unaccounted emotions in the place where the ghost resides
- unexplained smells such as that of sulfur or egg (very rare)

If you don't actually "see" a ghost but feel that there is one there (and you have eliminated all of the other things that are mistaken for ghosts), trust your feelings.

Word of Caution

Please do not attempt to clear ghosts and earthbound spirits without additional in-depth training. There are many good reasons for this warning. If you are interested in expanding your space clearing journey with this training, please visit www.InteriorAlignment.com.

ENERGY COMMONLY MISTAKEN FOR GHOSTS

While this book does not teach you how to release earthbound spirits and ghosts, it does provide you with the tools you need to clear a myriad of energies commonly believed to be ghosts.

The following energies are often mistaken for ghosts:

1. *Predecessor:* This is energy from a previous occupant. Over time, their energy permeated the space. For example, if the person who lived in the house died of a brain tumor and the new occupants begin to have severe headaches that they never had before, this might be predecessor energy. Most likely, this is not a ghost.

2. *Residual:* This is energy felt in a room after intense emotions (such as an argument, deep sadness, etc.). Someone might sleep in a bed and feel sad because the previous person who slept there felt sad.

3. *Elemental:* This is energy from the elemental kingdom—fairies, elms, gnomes, etc.—who may be angry or disgruntled. You might be walking in the woods and suddenly feel agitated for no apparent reason. The reason for this might be that the elementals in that area are not happy that you are in their space, or maybe there have been some disturbances (logging, construction, etc.) that are rousing them. Alternatively, you might also encounter joyous elementals. Almost always, elemental energy is in nature and not in home structures; however, there are exceptions to this.

4. *Astral:* You may meet astral beings when you are astral traveling. They are nonphysical, subtle energy life-forms that exist in the astral plane. There are a wide variety of these beings. Some are luminous and have a positive nature. Some are heavy or negative. These dense beings are called lower astral beings. For the most part, astral beings seem to have their own agendas, they like to keep to themselves, and they do not like being bothered. (You will almost never find an angel or a spirit guide in any of the astral levels. The vibration is too dense for them.)

There are an immense variety of beings in the astral plane. They were never human beings. In many ways they seem like creatures of the sea. They range from joyful, to helpful, to playful, to neutral, to mischievous, to mean-spirited . . . and to downright nasty. The astral plane can be likened to the ocean in which there are a vast variety of critters, such as dolphins, whales, sharks, angel fish, jellyfish, turtles, sea urchins, octopus, bivalves, and so on. Some of the ocean creatures seem pleasant and even amusing, such as a dolphin or a seal. Some are harmless, like sea turtles. Some are only harmful when disrupted, like an eel. Some can be harmful without doing it on purpose, such as stingrays. And others may seem menacing all the time, like sharks, even if they don't intend it. The astral level is filled with all categories of beings.

As a space clearer, it's valuable to know about the astral plane. However, unless you are an avid astral traveler in your dreams, normally you won't have many interactions in your life with these beings. The reason it's good to know about astral beings is because there are times when lower astral beings are attracted to strong emotions, and they can "glue" themselves or attach themselves to a person or a place on the earth plane.

For example, if you go into a bar and when you walk out you feel dirty, it could be that you have gotten an astral attachment. If you go shopping and then you have a terrible dream, it could be an astral attachment that you picked up from the shopping center. Often there are astral beings in hospitals, prisons, and mental institutions. Astral beings have a kind of consciousness and rarely— but sometimes—an awareness of what's around them, which is why they are often confused with ghosts. But they are not ghosts.

5. *Energy echoes:* Sometimes, when you walk into a place, it may feel like there are ghosts, but actually you have (partially) walked into a time warp. There are times, places, people, and events that can cause a spontaneous thinning of the veil between

the present, past, and future. When this occurs, everyone (who is sensitive to energy) can feel this. For example, many people may hear the battle cries from an ancient battlefield.

What is heard is a kind of echo from the past that everyone is picking up on. These do not need to be cleared. (However, you may be called to close the portal.)

6. *Karmic residue:* Sometimes there is only one individual who is aware of energy imprints from the past. It's like there is a veil between the part of you that is in the past life and the part of you that is here. For example, you might walk into a place where in a past life you were in battle and your head was bashed in, and now you have a horrible headache and memories arising. These images and feelings are not from ghosts. You are reexperiencing what happened in that life. Or you find yourself in a similar situation as one that you experienced in a past life and suddenly the feelings and images from that life arise. Again, this is not a ghost and doesn't need space clearing.

7. *Telepathic messages from the dead:* Sometimes a person will "see" someone who has recently passed on (for example, at the end of the bed), but these are not ghosts. These are messenger spirits who appear shortly after death to the people they love because they need to tell them something. They are aware of their death, and they often bring a message of comfort, saying they are well and to not grieve for them. Sometimes these spirits show themselves simply to notify a loved one of their passing, especially if they are a long distance away. They usually appear briefly and only one time. These are very common events.

8. *Telepathic messages from the living:* Another kind of telepathic message can come from someone who is living. The message/energy they send is so strong that it can feel like a ghost. They can either be trying to reach an individual and consciously sending energy, or they can be subconsciously sending strong emotions (either negative or positive) toward you. Sometimes protection/shielding is required.

9. *Crisis apparitions:* Sometimes there is a powerful psychic projection during a traumatic event. This usually only happens once. And this usually only occurs with a close relative or a very close friend. A mother sees her son at the exact time he is in a car accident. A wife sees her husband at the moment he has a heart attack. The person that appears is not always dead. A soldier in Iraq will appear to his mother, for instance; she will call and find out that her son has been shot and is in the hospital but is going to be okay.

10. *Object projections:* Sometimes strong energy radiates from objects that have absorbed psychic energy, which then projects out to people in the area. (An example of this is a mysterious object that would be locked in a room, and then the next day the room would be in huge disarray.) This is a kind of residual energy and is not attributed to ghosts.

11. *Energy tape loops:* These are energy imprints created by a strong event. They can play back over and over again like a tape loop. They are sometimes called "residual hauntings" or "spirit recordings." Sometimes they replay for an eternity. Maybe someone was very angry, and this energy continues to radiate into the space until it is cleared. Sometimes it can be an annual event that plays back at a particular time of year. Maybe it's a soldier looking out of a window in fear, or at the site of an accident. A traumatic moment can also leave an indelible mark on the building or area. This kind of so-called haunting is only a fragment or portion of the actual event. This is not a ghost.

12. *Psychic projections:* Sometimes a sensitive person will project images into a space as a response to residual telepathic energy in an area. (For example, it's possible for some people to project images onto photo film.) Additionally, some people will

unconsciously create a "ghost" psychic projection to satisfy their emotional needs.

13. *Poltergeist:* From the German words *poltern* and *geist*. *Poltern* means "noisy" and "mischievous." *Geist* means "spirit." Poltergeist activity includes loud sounds such as tapping or banging or displaced objects. Poltergeist is an uncontrollable psychokinetic energy from people with unresolved issues or suppressed emotions and is almost always generated from a teenager (or someone just entering puberty) that is emotionally suppressed.

A poltergeist differs from a ghost: Ghosts are most often perceived at night while poltergeist activity can happen any time. Ghosts are associated with a place. As a rule, ghosts don't change locations. Poltergeists are associated with a person and the activity follows the person if he or she moves. As a suggestion, if a house has poltergeist activity, suggest therapy with a qualified psychologist to address issues or emotions. This is *not* a case for space clearing or ghost clearing.

14. *Bi-location:* This is the spirit of a living person appearing to someone in a different location from where the living person actually is physically. The person whose spirit is seen is usually sleeping or meditating and is typically unaware of what is happening. This is not very common. However, highly spiritually attuned people, shamans, etc., can perform this at will.

15. *Psychological ghost phenomena:* This is an emotional projection, usually from a living person who is in emotional pain. For example, a grieving widow will insist that her dead husband is with her because she needs him to be there. She needs the comfort of knowing that his ghost is with her. She may subconsciously leave a door open and then later come upon it and declare that it is the ghost of her husband. You must be very careful not to disavow someone's reality; however, these "ghosts" are not real in any sense—they are just the conjuring of powerful imaginations.

16. *Aliens:* Sometimes an alien encounter is confused with a ghost encounter.

17. *Angels, spirit guides, spirit guardians, ancestors, spirits of the land, etc.:* If a person has a visitation from the higher spiritual realm of a land spirit, but it's an usual experience for that person, sometimes he or she becomes frightened and thinks that it was a ghost.

18. *Bad feng shui:* Sometimes what is simply "bad feng shui" can create a feeling of stagnation or heaviness, such as a dark, cramped space. But this is not a ghost.

About
the Author

Denise Linn's personal journey began as a result of a near-death experience at age 17. Her life-changing experiences and remarkable recovery set her on a spiritual quest that led her to explore the healing traditions of many cultures, including those of her own Cherokee ancestors, the Aborigines in the Australian bush, and the Zulus in Bophuthatswana. She trained with a Hawaiian kahuna (shaman) and Reiki Master Hawayo Takata. She was also ceremoniously adopted into a New Zealand Maori tribe. In addition, Denise lived in a Zen Buddhist monastery for more than two years.

Denise is an internationally renowned teacher in the field of self-development and has taught in 25 countries. She has written 19 books, which are available in 29 languages, including the bestseller *Sacred Space* and the award-winning *Feng Shui for the Soul*. Denise has appeared in numerous documentaries and television shows worldwide, and is the founder of the Red Lotus Woman's Mystery School, which offers professional certification programs. For information about Denise's certification programs and lectures, please visit her website: www.DeniseLinn.com.

HAY HOUSE TITLES OF RELATED INTEREST

YOU CAN HEAL YOUR LIFE, the movie, starring Louise Hay & Friends
(available as a 1-DVD program, an expanded
2-DVD set, and an online streaming video)
Learn more at www.hayhouse.com/louise-movie

THE SHIFT, the movie,
starring Dr. Wayne W. Dyer
(available as a 1-DVD program, an expanded
2-DVD set, and an online streaming video)
Learn more at www.hayhouse.com/the-shift-movie

*Clear Home, Clear Heart: Learn to Clear the Energy
of People and Places* by Jean Haner

Home in Harmony: Designing an Inspired Life
by Christa O'Leary

*Mantras in Motion: Manifesting What You Want
through Mindful Movement* by Erin Stutland

*What Your Clutter Is Trying to Tell You: Uncover the Message
in the Mess and Reclaim Your Life* by Kerri L. Richardson

All of the above are available at your local bookstore,
or may be ordered by contacting Hay House (see next page).

We hope you enjoyed this Hay House book. If you'd like to receive our online catalog featuring additional information on Hay House books and products, or if you'd like to find out more about the Hay Foundation, please contact:

Hay House, Inc., P.O. Box 5100, Carlsbad, CA 92018-5100
(760) 431-7695 or (800) 654-5126
(760) 431-6948 (fax) or (800) 650-5115 (fax)
www.hayhouse.com® • www.hayfoundation.org

———

Published in Australia by: Hay House Australia Pty. Ltd.,
18/36 Ralph St., Alexandria NSW 2015
Phone: 612-9669-4299 • *Fax:* 612-9669-4144
www.hayhouse.com.au

Published in the United Kingdom by: Hay House UK, Ltd.,
The Sixth Floor, Watson House, 54 Baker Street, London W1U 7BU
Phone: +44 (0)20 3927 7290 • *Fax:* +44 (0)20 3927 7291
www.hayhouse.co.uk

Published in India by: Hay House Publishers India,
Muskaan Complex, Plot No. 3, B-2, Vasant Kunj, New Delhi 110 070
Phone: 91-11-4176-1620 • *Fax:* 91-11-4176-1630
www.hayhouse.co.in

———

Access New Knowledge.
Anytime. Anywhere.

Learn and evolve at your own pace
with the world's leading experts.

www.hayhouseU.com